HOW TO PRAY

Metropolitan Youssef

ST MARY & MOSES ABBEY PRESS

How to Pray
By Metropolitan Youssef

Designed & Published by:
St. Mary & St. Moses Abbey Press
101 S Vista Dr, Sandia, TX 78383
stmabbeypress.com

Translation from Arabic by St. Mary & St. Moses Abbey.

Contents

Introduction

Prayer means "connection" or "communication," that is, a means of communication through which I make known to God my own request. God said, "Ask, and it will be given to you."[1] Therefore, I stand before Him and say, "Lord, I need such-and-such from You," or, "I would like to ask such-and-such from You," like what Samuel's mother Hannah did, and like what St. Mina the Wonderworker's mother Euphemia did.

Living lessons on prayer

In front of an icon of the Virgin, who is bearing Baby Jesus in her arms, the barren lady Euphemia stood, lifting her eyes to the face of the tender Mother. Her inner tears shattered her heart constricted by sorrow and pain, before they found their way to her eyes. In this state, she prayed to God that He may have compassion upon her and grant her a child.

---

1   Matthew 7:7.

She remained thus until she received the promise from God, through the icon of the Virgin, when she heard a voice coming from it, saying, "Amen." Therefore, she returned to her home in a completely different state. She returned joyful and rejoicing, fully confident in God's promise to her. For this reason, when she gave birth to her firstborn, she called him "Mena."

This story brings to mind another like it in the Old Testament, when Hannah, Samuel's mother, stood wrestling with God in the Temple, her soul bitter, asking Him the same request. And she was probably in the same state of sorrow, brokenness, and heartfelt tears. So her prayer was heard by God, and He confirmed that to her through the mouth of Eli the priest.[2]

Many of the saints also wrestled with God in prayer, like Jacob the patriarch, when he wrestled with God and held onto Him, saying, "I will not let You go unless You bless me!"[3] Daniel also sought the sympathy of God to hasten the ending of the captivity; and also Nehemiah, whose heart was stricken for the state of the walls of Jerusalem, which were broken and burnt with fire; and likewise others of the saints, the men of prayer.

Do you think, my beloved, that God did not know that Jacob wanted a blessing from Him, or

2   See 1 Samuel 1:1–18.

3   Genesis 32:26.

what was in Daniel's and Nehemiah's hearts? And did He not know that Hannah, Samuel's mother, desired to have a baby, or what Euphemia needed from Him? Of course God knew, but He said, "Ask, and it will be given to you; seek, and you will find; knock, and it will be opened to you."[4]

But if I say to myself, "God knows what I want and knows what I desire, so why should I pray? There is no point in praying. I will not ask God for anything, and if God wants to give it to me, He will. And if He does not want to give it to me, then He will not." My beloved, this understanding and conduct are not Christian at all. For the will of God is that we ask.

The Biblical approach to practicing the life of prayer

When a Christian is facing a difficult ordeal or some problem in their life, they sometimes become weak before it, or that their resoluteness breaks down, and they lose confidence in themselves and in God in whose hands are all things and who governs all things in all the creation.

Even if a person wants to seek God in their hardship and need, they often find that their mind is in turmoil, and they are perplexed: "How do I pray? What do I say?" The mind is scattered, half-

---

4   Matthew 7:7.

asleep, incapable of functioning, and the stress is enormous. Turmoil and anxiety overwhelm the person, and despair is about to engulf them. There is no clarity of mind, which would permit them to stand for prayer, and they feel that they are about to give up. They ask, "What do I do?"

Our teacher Paul the Apostle answers us and gives us direction in his epistle to the Philippians, saying, "Be anxious for nothing, but in everything by prayer and supplication, with thanksgiving, let your requests be made known to God."[5]

---

5   Philippians 4:6.

1

Be Anxious for Nothing

"Be anxious for nothing," meaning that a person does not worry nor is troubled for the sake of a problem or a request they have in their life. But can a person really be anxious for nothing in their life, while troubles and disturbances surround and trouble them continually? What are they supposed to do then? "… but in everything by prayer and supplication, with thanksgiving, let your requests be made known to God."[6]

How are our requests made known to God? Is He not the One who knows everything, and nothing can be hidden from Him? My brethren, when you have a problem in your life or a particular request, please do not be troubled nor worry about this matter. Rather, I would like you to present this request before God: "Let your requests be made

---

6   Ibid.

known to God." But how is it made known then? It is made known by prayer and thanksgiving, as our teacher Paul the Apostle says.

And does God, who sees everything and knows everything, not know my request, or is He not aware of it, but He asks me to make my request known to Him? Certainly not! Rather, God made prayer with thanksgiving as a suitable reaction for us, in the face of our problems and needs which we encounter in our lives. That is, this is the most suitable and guaranteed solution to the problems we fall into or when we are powerless before a request or need. Believe me, my beloved, that God made this for the sake of our goodness, our spiritual growth, and our inner peace at the same time.

When a person is suffering from a mental illness, and he continues to suppress his feelings and thoughts until he is about to explode, then, to save himself he decides to visit a psychiatrist. The first thing the doctor does is that he lets him talk and externalize all that is within him, even the requests which the doctor cannot and will not be able to fulfill for him. It suffices that he only listens to them, so that the balloon, which was about to explode, is deflated.

The problem here, however, is that as soon as he leaves the doctor, the balloon of the mind and thought will be re-inflated, and he will obtain neither peace nor the realization of their request.

As for us Christians, we have the King of peace, fully available to listen to us, twenty-four hours a day, seven days a week. He does not place upon us a condition of taking a prior appointment, and in addition, He is able to give us His peace freely. He is also able to answer our requests, no matter how impossible they may be. One of the fathers said concerning our tender-hearted God, "He silences the loud cries of the angels, to listen to the groaning of the man crying out to Him."

Then when you have a request or a problem, by prayer let your requests be made known before God. And as a result to this, "The peace of God, which surpasses all understanding, will guard your hearts and minds through Christ Jesus."[7]

And now, my beloved, after speaking about prayer and supplication with thanksgiving, we will finally speak about the result which surpasses comprehension and which is higher than the mind and understanding, capable of guarding our hearts and thoughts in Christ Jesus, and capable of keeping them secure against any demonic invasion and captivity—this result which is granted to us by prayer accompanied by thanksgiving.

As we have seen, the first advice St. Paul the Apostle gives us is that we should be anxious for nothing, and that we should not be troubled or disturbed. Do not be troubled or worry about any

---

7   Philippians 4:7.

problem in your life. Why? Being troubled and worrying mean that you lack faith and that you also care about the world. The Lord Christ often reproached his disciples, saying to them, "Why are you fearful, O you of little faith?"[8]

The person, who seeks God and who has a strong faith in Him, is not troubled, nor does he worry at all, though he is cast to the lions, though he is cast into the fiery furnace. This is because his faith is strong, immovable, his faith is stronger than the lions, and it surpasses the flames of fire in the intensity of its blazing. By his faith, he can stand before the most ferocious criminals and the most vicious, unrighteous judges. His faith can cast down the doubts sown by Satan and can pull down strongholds.[9] By his faith, he can confront the attractions of the world with all its pleasures, and he can rise above all his desires. "Though an army may encamp against me, my heart shall not fear; though war may rise against me, in this I will be confident."[10]

The person who believes in Christ also believes that He rose from the dead, and that he will rise like Him at His Second Coming. The Resurrection then is the essence of our faith, and it ought to occupy our minds always, and so we fear nothing. And nothing of this world, in which we are sojourners

8   Matthew 8:26.

9   See 2 Corinthians 10:4.

10   Psalms 27:3.

and strangers, can disturb our peace. We possess nothing of it, nor does it possess anything in us. All that we have currently is a gift which God has granted us, that we may use it according to His will, as faithful stewards. Our minds must be prepared to accept that it is God's right to reclaim what He has given us at any time, when the time of its use has come to an end.

As for being troubled and worried, which are contrary to faith, they are the thorns that choke both the person and the word of God within him, and so they cause him blight, sickness, and the loss of peace, but even worse they cause spiritual and eternal death.

Why do we, as Christians, forget this strong faith and become faint-hearted easily and continually? In the parable of the sower, the Lord Christ said to us that some seed fell among thorns, and when He explained this parable to His disciples, He made it clear to them that the thorns are a symbol of the cares of this world, the riches, and the pleasures.[11] These three things indicate that a person cares for the passing matters of the world. The person who always thinks, "What will we eat? What will we drink? What will we wear?" is a person who lives in anxiety, worry, and disturbance. I do not want to embarrass him further, nor make him fall into despair, by suggesting he has lost his faith. Rather, I

---

11   See Mark 4:19.

will encourage him and say to him that the lost faith can be restored once again, and that the one sleeping can wake up and arise from among the dead, so he sees the light of Christ, becomes enlightened by it, and lives forever.[12]

How then can he solve the problem of the loss of his faith, his many worries, and his disturbance? What can he do about this matter, rising once again? A person can resort to reading the word of God in the Holy Scriptures. But the thorns of disturbance and worry choke the word, preventing the person from bearing fruit. Therefore, the person must at first have faith that God answers. The matter is like a room with several doors and a fire set within it, but there is only one door for survival. The other doors, however, lead to being burned and to death.

We, Christians, know that there is only one door for survival and life, that is, the Lord Christ, "the door of the sheep."[13] This person, then, must walk through the right door, which is not only the door of survival, but also the door of joy and eternal life.

And if a person had faith that God would solve his problems and answer his requests, then he would not be troubled. "Which of you by worrying can add one cubit to his stature?"[14] So what benefit would he obtain from disturbance, worrying, and anxiety all

---

12   See Ephesians 5:14.

13   John 10:7.

14   Matthew 6:27.

day long? Let us my beloved, keep this in our hearts: when a person has a problem in their life, or has a request before God, they should not be troubled or worry, because worrying and being troubled make a person lose his peace. And this is a proof of his lack of faith.

Let us see St. Euphemia, the mother of the great martyr St. Mina. What did she do about her problem and request? She stood praying, fervently and with tears.

I want you, my beloved, to "be anxious for nothing, but in everything by prayer and supplication, with thanksgiving, let your requests be made known to God."[15] You can do nothing no matter how anxious you are. You might, of course, try on your own repeatedly, insistently, and stubbornly, but without Him you are deceived and receive something different from what you truly need; or perhaps you fail and fall into despair, or you may expose yourself to greater problems and consequently to more needs. But it is He who can do all things. He is God; therefore go to Him directly and do not waste your time in caring about other things which will not help you solve your problem.

Therefore, listen to what the Scripture says and do not be anxious about anything but rather pray and give thanks.

---

15   Philippians 4:6.

2

By Prayer and Supplication

God teaches us to ask: "Ask, and it will be given to you; seek, and you will find."[16] For if God gave us everything without asking, we would never learn how to make a single prayer.

When and how does a person learn to make prayers and supplications to God?

We can say that a person learns prayer when he enters into tribulation. As soon as a person enters into tribulation, he immediately begins praying with fervor. Then tribulation becomes a school that teaches prayer. Tribulation is the field in which a person kneels and prays before God. It is also the field through which a person hears the voice of God. It is the field in which we learn the arts of prayer, and we truly become men of prayer. God says to

16   Matthew 7:7.

every one of us, "Call upon Me in the day of trouble; I will deliver you, and you shall glorify Me."[17]

But, God, why do You allow that I suffer tribulation? Why do trials surround me, while I am Your son? I truly pray to You and have not ceased praying to You every day. Would it not be enough, Lord, that You allow tribulation only when I cease from praying to You?

Our fathers the pure Apostles answer our questions, as they learned from their Teacher, the Lord Christ.

St. Peter the Apostle says, "Beloved, do not think it strange concerning the fiery trial which is to try you, as though some strange thing happened to you."[18] St. Peter describes the tribulation as a fiery trial. That is, it stings, cauterizes, and is very painful. Nevertheless, it is very important for the sake of our testing; therefore, he calms us down and says that we should not think it strange or marvel. For this matter is not strange for us, Christians, because when we received the faith from Christ Himself, He said to us, "In the world you will have tribulation; but be of good cheer, I have overcome the world."[19]

But for what reason do You, Lord, test us? Are You not the One who looks at the heart from

---

17   Psalms 50:15.

18   1 Peter 4:12.

19   John 16:33.

within, searches the mind, and knows everything before they happen? My beloved, we are here on earth for the sake of the entrance test to eternal life. As an elementary school student passes the elementary school test, which is easy, and then he advances gradually until he reaches the university test, which is very difficult, so does God make us advance gradually and lifts us up, from one degree to another, until we enter eternal life, pure. Therefore, we should not marvel, as though some strange thing happened, as our teacher St. Peter the Apostle said to us.

St. James the Apostle also said, "My brethren, count it all joy when you fall into various trials."[20] There are also several kinds of trials at the same time. Would this not be too much for us, causing us to suffer failure, sorrow, and disturbance? It is impossible that God, who knows us better and more precisely than we do ourselves, would give trials or a trial to a person that is beyond his ability to endure. Rather, with the trial He gives the way of escape and the suitable solution.[21] Therefore, St. James the Apostle commands us to rejoice when the Lord permits us to fall into various trials at the same time. This is the proof of His trust in us, His great love for us, His care for our spiritual growth and progress, so that we may all the more come close to Him. He draws us away slowly from the matters

---

20   James 1:2.

21   See 1 Corinthians 10:13.

of the world and its passing attractions, to prepare us and make us kings and priests in His eternal kingdom. "For whom the LORD loves He chastens, and scourges every son whom He receives,"[22] "just as a father the son in whom he delights."[23]

Concerning this St. Luke the Apostle says, "We must through many tribulations enter the kingdom of God."[24] "But, Lord, is it not sufficient that there are several kinds of tribulations and trials, so why should they be 'many' at the same time?" My beloved, if any of us sees one minute of eternity, he will undoubtedly long to go through more tribulations. Then you, the chosen by God, blessed are you, because you are commended in heaven.

St. Paul the Apostle also said, "For our light affliction, which is but for a moment, is working for us a far more exceeding and eternal weight of glory."[25] Paul, do you not feel the difficulty of the tribulation I am in, that you would describe it as light and transient, but in reality it is very heavy, and it even seems heavier than what I can endure. Also, time is not able to tell when it will end; that is, all the indications say that it will remain for years and years!

My beloved children, what is the number of

---

22 Hebrews 12:6.

23 Proverbs 3:12.

24 Acts 14:22.

25 2 Corinthians 4:17.

years of our life on earth? Has anyone been able to theoretically count the number of years of eternity? If we looked to the tribulation through the perspective of the earth and what is in it, we would find it to be very heavy in truth, extending to a length which is difficult for the heart and soul to accept and endure patiently. But if we looked to the tribulation through a perspective that is heavenly, eternal, we would see the tribulation as it really is—light and transient. And as our teacher Pope Shenouda III said, "It is bound to end. It is all for the good."

Let us use this heavenly perspective always, so that we may not lose our peace by ourselves, without anybody trying to take it away from us. All that St. Paul did, to give us a true view of the kingdom and the glory of eternity, is that he exchanged before our eyes the two scales of the balance. So, instead of the weight being placed upon us, to weigh down our shoulders and make us suffer pain in the depths of our souls, he turned it to the other side, to tilt the weight of our burden to there in eternity, thereby deepening our foundations in it and making our glory there more magnificent. Or, to say it more correctly, the Apostle corrected for us the erroneous state of the balance, which is of our making, into the right state.

Concerning tribulations, St. John the Apostle said, "These are the ones who come out of the great tribulation, and washed their robes and made them white in the blood of the Lamb."[26] He also said, "I, John, both your brother and companion in the tribulation and kingdom and patience of Jesus Christ."[27] Is it not enough that the disciple whom the Lord Jesus loved the most, not only is our companion in the great tribulation which we are passing through, but also because of our endurance and patience he calls us his brethren and companions with him in the kingdom of our Lord Jesus?

He saw us beforehand, in a prophetic vision outside the frame of time, victorious, coming out of our great tribulation, wearing white robes which are washed in the pure blood of Christ. And the rest is indescribable. So what greater consolation do we have more than this?

For the sake of this, without exaggeration, we cannot but say, "How beautiful and how sweet are you, tribulations! For you are the treasure we store up for our other life after this fleeting life which quickly evaporates. We thank you, also, for how many times because of you we offered requests and prayers, with hot tears which were as a balm on the wounds of our Savior. And when you were so kind as to visit us, we arose to meet you with prayer to God, and He answered us, and we made for ourselves a sweet remembrance, which cannot be erased, in His tender heart inclining toward us. And we sang

---

26   Revelation 7:14.

27   Revelation 1:9.

with our voices, a sweet and pleasant hymn which delighted His ears, exactly like what we learned from our sweet teacher, David the psalmist in his psalms, 'In my distress I called upon the LORD, and cried out to my God; He heard my voice from His temple, and my cry entered His ears.'[28] Therefore, 'I love the LORD, because He has heard my voice and my supplications. Because He has inclined His ear to me, therefore I will call upon Him as long as I live.'[29]"

Someone who has experienced efficacy of prayer during tribulations said, "Pray fervently in your tribulation, and be strong and of good courage, for tribulations make strong men." Do this that you may become a man of prayer, strong, courageous, healthy in soul and spirit.

---

28 2 Samuel 22:7.
29 Psalms 116:1–2.

3

With Thanksgiving

The third point which St. Paul the Apostle addressed is "with thanksgiving." We often call God in tribulation, and the Lord always delivers us, but very rarely do we glorify Him and go back to thank Him through prayer. Therefore, St. Paul the Apostle says, "In everything by prayer and supplication, with thanksgiving, let your requests be made known to God."[30] He also said in his epistle to the Ephesians, "giving thanks always."[31] St. Paul links between prayer and thanksgiving, for as he says, "pray without ceasing,"[32] he also says, "giving thanks always."

So, how does a person pray always and give thanks always at the same time? If I presented a request before God, and He answered me, I rejoice

---

30   Philippians 4:6.

31   Ephesians 5:20.

32   1 Thessalonians 5:17.

in this; and when I am joyful, I give thanks. So how do I thank God? I thank Him by praying to Him. Then thanksgiving is prayer. Prayer leads to joy, and joy leads to thanksgiving, and thanksgiving leads to prayer. And through this way is fulfilled the saying, "Pray always, give thanks always, and also rejoice always."[33]

St. Isaac the Syrian says, "Nor does any gift remain without addition, save that which is received without thanksgiving."[34]

When do we give thanks?

David the prophet says in the psalm, "Why are you so sad, O my soul? And why do you trouble me? Hope in God, for I will give thanks to Him; my God is the salvation of my countenance."[35] It is clear that David here was crying out to God during a severe tribulation he was suffering, but he thanked God for His salvation which he had not yet received. This is truly the greatest degree of thanksgiving, that we give thanks before we receive the answer.

The same thing happened with Jonah the prophet, while he was in the belly of the fish, where he prayed, saying, "But I will sacrifice to You

---

33   Cf. 1 Thessalonians 5:16–18. "Rejoice always, pray without ceasing, in everything give thanks."

34   *The Ascetical Homilies of Saint Isaac the Syrian.* (Boston, MA: Holy Transfiguration Monastery, 2011), 120.

35   Psalms 42:5 LXX, Orthodox Study Bible (OSB).

with the voice of thanksgiving; I will pay what I have vowed. Salvation is of the LORD."[36] It is truly marvelous that Jonah cried out with the voice of thanksgiving at the pinnacle of his tribulation and suffering, in a place like a grave, while his fate was unknown and dark—at depths no man had entered nor passed through before him!

The Church also teaches us to pray with thanksgiving, for all the liturgical prayers start with the Thanksgiving Prayer: "Let us give thanks to the beneficent and merciful God..." And this is the case in all the occasions: the Eucharist, the Crowning Prayer, even the Funeral Prayer for the departed. The Church has set the Thanksgiving Prayer at the beginning of every prayer.

We should then give thanks at all times, always, for if we reflect, we will find a great many things to thank and glorify God for, and we rejoice always at the same time. For the prayer of thanksgiving is both a mother and daughter of joy at the same time. God's will for us is that we rejoice; therefore, Paul the Apostle continues to teach us the sound and joyful Christian life, after he commands us to serve one another to fulfill the law of love,[37] saying, "Rejoice always, pray without ceasing, in everything give thanks; for this is the will of God in Christ Jesus for you."[38]

---

36   Jonah 2:9.

37   See 1 Thessalonians 5:13–15.

38   1 Thessalonians 5:16–18.

But, unfortunately, many of us seek refuge in grumbling, although God has given us exceedingly many gifts and outstanding talents too. But they stop at something small and trivial, feeling they lack it, so they start to grumble and feel distressed. Sadly, they are far away from the spirit of thanksgiving, and by this they bring upon themselves psychological illnesses and cover their spirits with utter darkness.

In order that we may distinguish our internal state, whether we are living the true life of thanksgiving or not, we can compare between the states of the human soul through its internal and external reactions when one is going through a trial or tribulation.

1. The complaining person. This person complains always, for everything, and grumbles concerning everything. He must look for fault in everything that is before him, and declare it to the crowd, and exaggerate exceedingly in describing every fault and shortcoming.

All his words are grumbling and complaining, with no aim. In his continuous complaining, he talks about men, animals, insects, and the conditions in their various kinds, whether political conditions, or economical, or monetary, or even the familial and personal conditions. But even inanimate objects do not escape his excessive complaining.

If he walks with you outdoors, you find him say, "What is this terrible hot weather?" or he might say, "This cold weather is horrible and extremely intolerable!" There is no midway with him. It is very difficult that he likes anything or that he is satisfied with any condition. He always finds room for complaining at all times, and nothing strikes his liking.

This poor person, after his relatives and friends bear with him for a time, they begin distancing themselves from him and avoiding him, so that they may not contract his psychological afflictions, and so that the gloominess of his spirit may not be transmitted to them. He harms himself from within first, and often he falls into despair, but if the matter progresses further with him, without him trying to treat himself, he might think of committing suicide. Here the necessity of his treatment by a specialist is made manifest.

Let us beware then lest much complaining lead us to dangerous stages, if we leave it thus with no true, spiritual treatment. And at the same time, we should be confident and assured that the treatment for this case is absolutely guaranteed in Christ, and the most important step for treatment is becoming accustomed to prayer and thanksgiving.

2. The clever person. The personality of this one is slightly better than the previous, for when he faces a problem or falls into a particular trial, he looks for a suitable person to talk to concerning his trial or problem. This is not for the purpose of complaining, but it is so that he may ask for guidance and advice, to solve his problem or to help him come out of his trial. He pursues to reap benefit from the experience of others, in what he himself has not experienced or passed through before. He does not calm down until he finds a solution for his problem, or at least how he may adapt to it or deal with it wisely. And back in the day, we used to hear a folk maxim that says, "The complainer moans and says, 'Why?' and the clever is diligent and says, 'What do I do?'"

3. The thankful person. This person's personality is much better than the aforementioned two. When he is going through a tribulation or trial, he quickly seeks God and thanks Him in prayer. Believe me, my beloved, this person is full of inner joy. In this way thanksgiving is a prayer, and prayer is thanksgiving. Thanksgiving is not a mere passing word with which we suppose that we thanked God and that is all. Therefore, my beloved, if we always enjoy the spirit of thanksgiving, it will definitely lead us to praying from the heart.

4

The Conditions for an Answered Prayer

For a prayer to be powerful and for the answer to come, prayer needs the following five fundamental conditions.

1. A Quiet Place

Because of the importance of this condition, the Lord Christ teaches in the Gospel according to St. Matthew, saying, "But you, when you pray, go into your room, and when you have shut your door, pray to your Father who is in the secret place."[39] Many of us think that "go into your room" is a phrase that has a symbolic meaning, with no literal meaning intended by it. Nevertheless, there are many sayings

---

39   Matthew 6:6.

which the Lord Christ said, by which He meant the literal and true meaning, and they do not carry in their essence any other symbolic meaning, save the literal meaning which they indicate clearly.

The Lord Christ said this and meant by it the literal and true meaning, where during prayer a person should stay away from any source of noise, so that he may be able to pray quietly. For if you tried to pray in a place that is not quiet, it would be very difficult for you to concentrate on prayer.

The Holy Scripture informs us of the Lord Christ's approach in prayer, where it says, "He went up on the mountain by Himself to pray."[40] Why does the Lord Christ go to the mountain to pray? The mountain is the quiet place, a place where the Lord is alone for the sake of prayer to God the Father. The mountain was a suitable place, away from any disturbance.

Likewise we also necessarily need to prepare a suitable place for prayer in our homes. Unfortunately, we often prepare for this purpose an unsuitable corner between the television and the computer, and other amenities and home appliances which give rise to noise and distraction. For a person needs a quiet place, to be able to focus and forget everything and not to turn around to anything nearby. We can prepare such a place at home, where it may be truly quiet, far away from any source causing noise and

---

40   Matthew 14:23.

distraction.

On this occasion, I would like to indicate that often when I am visiting homes, it pains me on the inside to find no Christian icons nor any pictures of saints, all the while the house instead is full of worldly pictures, of actors and actresses, and other decorative objects. All this expresses the culture and care of the owner of the home. Should we not be proud of our Christianity and seek the help of the cloud of witnesses who are interceding for our sakes always, and who would like to help us pass through the world where we are strangers, and to share with them in the inheritance of the heavenly glory as the one body of Christ?

When we prepare a place specified for prayer, we should completely clear it of any worldly pictures. Foremost, we should place an icon of the Lord Christ, and our prayers to God the Father should be lifted up through His holy name. We should also adorn it, as is available, with icons of angels and saints, that we may seek their help, blessing, and intercession during our struggle in prayer. It would also be great if we placed a vigil lamp or a candle stand, and we persisted in lighting it and caring for it, that it may be a continual reminder that we should pray. I know that some godly families make this place as though it were a part of church; therefore, they take off their shoes before entering and do not allow any family member to bring in food or drink, to eat and drink in it. Rather they treat it with respect and reverence like the sanctuary in church.

Let us imagine together what impact this would have on little children when they are raised in a home like this.

2. A Designated Time

New habits and behaviors have become widespread these days among believers concerning prayer. For example, some of us often turn to prayer during driving a car, or while walking to work or from work, or even during work itself, or during the preparation of food or any other housework.

It is good for a person to pray always as the Holy Scripture commands us, but it is not good that this be the only time for prayer, and that this be the only way for prayer. There must necessarily be a designated time for prayer, as there should also be a designated place for prayer.

When I have an important matter and I need to make this matter known to God, is it fitting that I speak with God on this important matter while I am preoccupied with many other things I am doing at the same time? I absolutely need to designate time for this important matter, and also need a quiet place suitable for this purpose.

Tell me, brethren, can you, for example, take a shower on your way to work? Unfortunately, you do have a designated time for taking a shower, and a special place also for this purpose. Nevertheless, you complain that you neither have time nor a designated place for prayer.

Also, when you are having a conversation with a friend or anyone on the phone, then this person feels that you are not giving him your attention during the conversation, so he asks you, "Why are you not paying attention to me? Are you busy?" You answer him, saying, "Yes, I am busy, indeed." He says to you, "Give me only a few minutes of your time, so that I can talk with you. Please give me some of your attention." Similarly, when you are speaking with someone who is reading a newspaper and who does not want to lift his eyes from it to you, to listen to you, you feel that this person is paying you no attention. So you say to yourself that since this person is paying me no attention, I cannot talk with him. Also I will not sit again with him. Do you want God to say the same words about you?

The same thing exactly could happen with respect to the one who prays only while driving the car, cooking the food, or during any other daily routine duties. Therefore, there must also be a designated time and a quiet place for prayer.

Of the necessary things also is the commitment to this time and greatly respecting it, as is fitting of the position and reverence of the Person owning it, more than any other person or thing in this world. For example, when we visit a monastery, the monks in this monastery have a gathering to pray the Vespers Prayer at five in the evening every day. And about ten minutes before the appointed time for prayer, you find all of them have left their works, meetings, and whatever is in their hands, heading to church for the prayer gathering.

Likewise we also, if we did not right away abandon everything that is in our hands before the appointed time for prayer by a sufficient period of time, heading to the place designated for prayer, it would be very easy for the devil to entice us into exchanging prayer for something else. And at the end of the day, we find that we have become distracted by preoccupations, and we are barely capable of moving our body which is overburdened by fatigue and weariness, having no energy. So in this day we lose the method of our connection with God our Creator. And if we do not quickly become alert to this mistake and fall, perhaps this matter might recur, turning into a habit that persists for a long time, causing us catastrophic eternal and spiritual losses.

3. Prayer Needs Words

It often happens that a person stands to pray yet he does not know what he will say during prayer.

All the traditional churches have what is called a prayer book, not only our Coptic Church, and it is usually called "The Book of Hours," which is called in Coptic "The Agpeya." It consists of psalms, which were given by God; therefore, they are God's words, because they were inspired by God Himself.

As our bodies require a nutritional meal to eat, that they may live and not die, so are the psalms of the Hours are the nutritional meal which our spirits require, to live and to be invigorated and to not die. As the weeping prophet Jeremiah said, "Your words were found, and I ate them, and Your word was to me the joy and rejoicing of my heart."[41]

Not only do the words of God in the psalms include rich food, but they also include the delicious sweets which delight the heart and spirit more and more, as the psalmist David says in the psalm, "How sweet are Your words to my taste, sweeter than honey to my mouth!"[42]

Then in the Agpeya, we pray with the words of God, which were inspired by Him, and therefore, our prayers are prayers of the Lord, according to His will and desire. Then comes the personal prayer, according to our ability, yet it is derived from the words of God which were inspired in the psalms; that is, they are considered as an echo of the words of God, which the Holy Spirit, who is working in us, guides us to. Otherwise, our prayer becomes as St. James said, "You ask and do not receive, because

---

41   Jeremiah 15:16.
42   Psalms 119:103.

you ask amiss, that you may spend it on your pleasures."[43]

4. Prayer Needs a Teacher

The disciples asked the Lord Christ, saying, "Lord, teach us to pray, as John also taught his disciples."[44] Who then teaches us prayer?

The disciples were passionate about being like their Teacher, our Lord Jesus Christ, whom they saw always, withdrawing from people and going alone to pray. For He did not command them, nor us, anything at all which He Himself did not do. Then after He gave them the Lord's prayer, "Our Father in heaven,"[45] which is like a treasure of the treasures of all prayers, He explained to them in the course of His words that this holy prayer is only the introduction of prayer and its conclusion. As for applying its meaning and its purpose, this includes the whole day, but even the whole life, meaning that through it we may have a permanent connection with God. And for the sake of learning this connection and preserving its continuation, a permanent guide or teacher is required, to teach us and guide us to that which is in agreement with it and falls under its context; while he forbids us and warns us of that which is contrary to it and deviates from it.

---

43 James 4:3.
44 Luke 11:1.
45 Luke 11:2.

Because the Lord knew that, after He accomplished the death on the cross and redemption, He would ascend to heaven, He said to His disciples, "And I will pray the Father, and He will give you another Helper, that He may abide with you forever—the Spirit of truth, whom the world cannot receive, because it neither sees Him nor knows Him; but you know Him, for He dwells with you and will be in you."[46] Then after the Lord had reassured His disciples that the Comforter will dwell always within them, He revealed to them who this permanent Comforter is, saying, "But the Helper, the Holy Spirit, whom the Father will send in My name, He will teach you all things, and bring to your remembrance all things that I said to you."[47] Then our Teacher who dwells always with us and in us, is the Holy Spirit, and He is the one who preserves our unceasing connection with God: "For we do not know what we should pray for as we ought, but the Spirit Himself makes intercession for us with groanings which cannot be uttered."[48]

I wish that we do not quench the Holy Spirit within us at any time,[49] nor grieve Him,[50] lest our relationship with God be disrupted.

As we said concerning the personal prayer which

---

46   John 14:16–17.

47   John 14:26.

48   Romans 8:26.

49   See 1 Thessalonians 5:19.

50   See Ephesians 4:30.

the Holy Spirit teaches us, putting the words in our hearts and mouths, whose foundation are the words of God, so also does the Spirit teach us how to walk in wisdom in our whole life: "redeeming the time, because the days are evil."[51] And this is the case after we persevere in all the means of grace. That is to say, through the Holy Spirit we form an unceasing connection with God, feeling His presence always, so that the saying of the psalmist is applied to us, "But I give myself to prayer."[52]

Let us then submit to our Teacher, the Holy Spirit, and let us not disobey Him by obeying the desires of our bodies, Satan's enticements, and choosing the pleasures of this world instead of His counsels and His directions in our hearts.

5. Prayer Needs Determination

How many times does a person have a longing for prayer, yet does not do it out of laziness? Or he may be preoccupied with other things? How many times did you feel that you longed to pray, but then you said to yourself, "Let me finish this thing, then I will pray." Afterwards, in the end, as soon as you finish the thing you were doing, you find yourself drowsy, so you barely pray "Our Father" in haste before going to sleep.

---

51 Ephesians 5:16.
52 Psalms 109:4.

Therefore, we reiterate what St. Paul the Apostle says, "Be anxious for nothing, but in everything by prayer,"[53] meaning that you should make prayer your first concern always.

Prayer needs determination and needs a true struggler who struggles in prayer. No obstacles hinder him, whether bodily, psychological, worldly, or even spiritual obstacles. Regarding this, one of the fathers says, "You are not responsible for the success, but for the struggle."

If you grow feeble because of your feeling of failure in any spiritual matter or virtue, make sure that your determination does not become weak, and you abandon your prayers.

Not only is the firm determination important for the perseverance in prayer, but it is also the strong fort of the will, which makes the soul pass by all kinds of offenses and weaknesses, especially the remembrance of evil and old habits. These the enemy tries to revive in us again, whenever he smells in us a hint of the smell of laziness and slackness, or whenever we give him an entrance by ceasing from the life of spiritual watchfulness and by giving in to distraction of thoughts and daydreaming.

The following saying by one of the fathers may be of great help to us during our prayers, so that our thought may not be distracted: "It is very dangerous, even fatal, to give in to distraction of

---

53   Philippians 4:6.

thought and wandering of mind, so if your thoughts wander away from you during prayer, go back and gather them again, and restore them so that they may stand once again before Christ the King."

This struggle needs a strong determination from you, and patience with longsuffering. No matter how many times you fall, do not ever fall into despair, but remember that you are in a state of continual war with the powers of darkness, and cry out in the face of every weakness and every sin, saying, "Do not rejoice over me, my enemy; when I fall, I will arise; when I sit in darkness, the LORD will be a light to me."[54]

He who becomes weak and falls, let him not postpone his repentance, lest he wallow more in sin and his determination become weaker. Also, let him not be ashamed, because of his sin, to offer his prayer to God in its appointed time, even if this were after falling into sin immediately, claiming that his mind and conscience have become defiled, and it would not be fitting for him to stand before God and lift up his hands to heaven. These, my brother, are demonic thoughts, with which the devil dominates you through his cunning, so that you may not run away from him quickly. Rather remember that the father embraced his prodigal son while he was still in his filthy clothes, from which the stench of pigs emanated. Likewise, a mother is not repulsed at all

---

54   Micah 7:8.

by cleaning her soiled little baby, nor at his smell. In like manner, God is not repulsed by our filthiness and our unclean actions, no matter how bad they are, with the condition that we lift up our hearts to Him in prayer and say to Him with true repentance, "I have sinned against heaven and in your sight, and am no longer worthy to be called your son."[55]

The following story is related in *The Paradise of the Monks*:

It was said concerning a brother who was living in a monastery, that from the intensity of the battle he used to many times fall into fornication. He remained forcing himself and enduring, lest he leave his monastic schema. And he used to perform his rule and his [prayers of the] Hours with care, saying in his prayer, "Lord, You see the severity of my state and sorrow; therefore, rescue me, Lord, whether I desire it or not, because I am like mire, I long and love sin, but You are the mighty God. Stop me from this uncleanness. For if You had mercy on the saints only, this would not be marvelous; and if You saved the chaste, what would be the need, for those are worthy? But in me, I who am unworthy, show the greatness of Your mercy, Master, for I have surrendered myself to You." This is what he said daily,

---

55   Luke 15:21.

whether or not he sinned. But one day, while he was unceasingly praying this, the devil, having become weary of his good hope and his praise-worthy boldness[56], he appeared to him face to face, while he was chanting his psalms, and said to him, "Are you not ashamed to stand in the hands of God and to call His name with your unclean mouth?" The brother said to him, "Do you give me a blow with a sledgehammer, and I give you a blow with a sledgehammer? You make me fall into sin, and I beseech the merciful God to have compassion on me. For I fight with you in this struggle until death overtakes me, and I do not cut off my hope in my God and do not cease from readying myself for you. And we will see who will overcome: you or the mercy of God?" Therefore, when the devil heard his words, he said, "From now on I will not fight you, lest I be a reason for you receiving crowns on your hope in your God."[57]

Unfortunately, many had a good beginning with Christ, but then they cooled off and backslid, or fell

---

56   Literally: impudence.

57   *Bostan Al-Rohban* [Paradise of the Monks], Bishop Epiphanius, ed. (Cairo, Egypt: Dar Majalat Marcus, 2014), 293. [Translated from Arabic text]. Cf. *The Anonymous Sayings of the Desert Fathers*, J. Wortley, trans. (Cambridge, UK: Cambridge University Press, 2013), N.582.

into despair and stopped following Him,[58] but the boast of the saints is their strong determination and their longsuffering in everything, and by these they were counted as saints.

---

58   See John 6:66.

5

Important Directions During Prayer

As there are five principal conditions for prayer, so are there also five important directions that must be observed when standing during prayer.

1. Humbly pour yourself out before Him

As St. Paul said, "In everything by prayer and supplication, with thanksgiving…"[59] It is as though he wants to say to us, "Prayer is the means for conveying our words and requests to God."

When we offer our prayers before God humbly, He hears us. Hannah poured herself out before God humbly, and God heard and gave her Samuel. The same thing happened with St. Euphemia, and God

59   Philippians 4:6.

heard her and gave her St. Mina.

Therefore, in the Divine Liturgy, when we stand before God to present our requests to Him, the priest says on our behalf in the litanies, "Again, let us ask God the Pantocrator, the Father of our Lord, God, and Savior Jesus Christ. We ask and entreat Your goodness, O Lover of Mankind…" Through it, we set our hope in God and implore Him; therefore, the priest does not stand proudly in the middle before the Altar, but he stands with a contrite heart, as though imploring on the side of the Altar. And in the Prayer of Preparation, he prays, saying, "I do not have the countenance to draw near and open my mouth before Your holy glory."

We can give a simile to this. It is like a beggar who asks with contrition, a lowered head, and a humble heart. He stretches his hands out, hoping and entreating, that he may find someone to have compassion on him and give him alms. This is exactly as David did, for he said, "Hear the voice of my supplications when I cry to You, when I lift up my hands toward Your holy sanctuary."[60] He also presents an urgent appeal for help, as though he were in danger, having no one to deliver him, except for God. And we can consider "before Your holy glory" as directing our hearts to heaven, while the lifting up of the hands is like Moses, who stood lifting up his hands in the likeness of the cross, entreating for

---

60   Psalms 28:2.

the sake of the deliverance of the children of Israel through the leadership of Joshua.

Likewise we ought to be in a state of entreaty and contrition, lifting up our hands, when seeking something from our heavenly Father. For this reason also, we ought to always preserve the beautiful habit which we received from our fathers, of lifting up our hands and directing our eyes to heaven whenever we pray the Lord's Prayer, "Our Father." Some, unfortunately, began to neglect this habit which indicates humility.

2. Ask with persistence

Persistence does not issue except from a heart that has no one to help it, but only the one it is seeking refuge in, like the widow who went to the unjust judge, to get justice from her adversaries. And for the sake of her persistence, he heard her. Yes, only for the sake of her persistence, and not because he feared God or regarded anyone, nor even because he feared for his reputation. The Lord Christ said, "Hear what the unjust judge said. And shall God not avenge His own elect who cry out day and night to Him, though He bears long with them?"[61]

After the Lord Jesus delivered to us the crown of all our prayers, that is, the Lord's Prayer, He did not stop at this. Rather, so that we may continue

---

61   Luke 18:6–7.

laboring throughout our lives in what this prayer means, and may comprehend what it ought to do in us through what follows it, the Lord Jesus related to us the parable of the friend who came at midnight. He came knocking at his friend's door at midnight, asking him for three loaves of bread, for he was surprised by the visit of his friend who came from a long journey. The duty of hospitality necessitated that he prepared a table for him. People at that time, for the sake of keeping warm, used to sleep on one bed, for he said to him, "Do not trouble me; the door is now shut, and my children are with me in bed; I cannot rise and give to you."[62] Also, the doors at that time were huge, with latches and primitive iron locks, which make disturbing noise when they are opened and closed. This means that everyone in the house would inevitably be awakened from sleep. Nevertheless, the Lord confirmed the result to us at the end of the story, saying, "Because of his persistence he will rise and give him as many as he needs."[63]

Then He gave us the famous principle of prayer, which St. Anthony the Great, the father of monks, took as a motto for himself, "Ask, and it will be given to you; seek, and you will find; knock, and it will be opened to you. For everyone who asks receives, and he who seeks finds, and to him who

---

62   Luke 11:7.

63   Luke 11:8.

knocks it will be opened."[64]

What prevents you then from making God a friend of yours, importuning Him through a boldness stemming from your long companionship with Him and from being always in contact with Him? Therefore, you should not feel ashamed to ask Him for anything for the sake of your loved ones and friends, at a suitable time and an unsuitable time, like a friend in the middle of the night, and even if your requests were strange and may appear impossible according to men's understanding, and even if perhaps no one has ever asked for them before you did.

St. Macarius the Great says in one of his renowned homilies:

> But when the Lord sees that to the best of its ability the soul recollects itself, always seeking and waiting for the Lord night and day, and crying to Him, even as He commanded to "pray without ceasing in everything,"[65] He will avenge it, as He promised, cleansing it from the evil within it, and will present it unto Himself a bride without blemish and without spot[66].[67]

---

64   Luke 11:9–10.

65   1 Thessalonians 5:17.

66   See Ephesians 5:27

67   *Fifty Spiritual Homilies of St. Macarius the Egyptian*, A.J. Mason, trans. (London, UK: Society for Promoting Christian Knowledge,

As we have previously said, the Lord has not commanded us to do anything which He Himself did not do. Therefore, let us always remember the way He looked when He prayed persistently. It was said concerning His prayer in the garden, that He prayed "more earnestly" and with a great struggle, that is, there is no greater or lesser measure of persistence[68] than this. And because of this persistence "His sweat became like great drops of blood falling down to the ground."[69] All this is for your sake and mine, because we are His bride, and His love for us is indescribable. During His struggle in praying "more earnestly," which is attainable by all mankind, His exceedingly great love made His sweat be as drops of blood that water and soften the earth beneath Him—it is truly love unto death!

God loves your persistence, for it confirms and proves the great degree of your attachment to Him, and your hope in Him alone, and your faith in His power and ability, and your trust that He hears you. All these are of the essentials of the true and constant love for God. For this reason, the psalmist used to importune God always in his psalms, saying, "O You who hear prayer, to You all flesh will come."[70]

1921), 241.

68   The Arabic word is the same as that which appears as "earnestly" in NKJV.

69   Luke 22:44.

70   Psalms 65:2.

3. Pray with Tears

St. John Climacus says, "If God in His love for mankind had not given us tears, those being saved would be few indeed and hard to find."[71]

David entreats God, saying, "All night I make my bed swim; I drench my couch with my tears,"[72] "And mingled my drink with weeping."[73] Then he demands that God should keep these tears with Him, knowing through the Holy Spirit that God will not forget them at all, and he is certain that they will be preserved: "Put my tears into Your bottle; are they not in Your book?"[74] while the Bridegroom, the Lord, responds to His bride, the human soul, saying, "Turn your eyes away from me, for they have overcome me."[75] Do you see how tears are the thing that can overcome God?

How, however, do I acquire the grace of praying with tears? Praying with tears is indeed a grace given by the Holy Spirit. It originates from a faithful heart, fervent in spirit and the love for the Bridegroom Christ. It also originates spontaneously and is unfeigned and unintentional. It results from faithfulness in the spiritual struggle and the fervor in

---

71   Saint John Climacus, *The Ladder of Divine Ascent.* (Boston, MA: Holy Transfiguration Monastery, 2019), 112.

72   Psalms 6:6.

73   Psalms 102:9.

74   Psalms 56:8.

75   Song of Solomon 6:5.

prayer, especially during hardships and tribulations, and also during the pinnacle of divine consolations or for the sake of the joy in Christ. It also occurs when the Lord reveals to the soul divine mysteries and exceeding visions.

Concerning this, Pope Shenouda III says, "Be faithful regarding prayer with understanding and fervor, and God will raise you to prayer with tears."[76] He who is faithful with what is least, God will make him ruler over much.[77] When God sees your struggle and forcefulness in prayer from the depths of your heart, and your relentless attempts to control your thoughts which desire to wander, then He will grant you the grace of tears. Then He will say to you, "I have heard your prayer, I have seen your tears."[78]

For tears are truly the daughter of prayer, and the sister of supplication, requesting, and begging for help.

The greatest source of tears which the saints, the desert ascetics, used is weeping for sins. It is a source out of which abundant tears spring forth, for everyone who offers a true repentance with all their heart, feeling sorry for their sins, which caused all these sufferings to their compassionate Redeemer, portraying His wound before them and His open

---

76   His Holiness Pope Shenouda III, *Ma'alim Al-tareik Al-rohei* [Landmarks on the Spiritual Path]. (Cairo, Egypt: The Theological College for the Coptic Orthodox, 1987), 152. [Translated from Arabic].

77   See Luke 16:10.

78   Isaiah 38:5.

side by the spear of their sins.[79] Therefore, you can do nothing but weep and shed tears.

They are the tears of regret for the lost time in entertainment and the false happiness in the vain pleasures of the world. They are also the tears of forgiveness and remission, as a captive asking the king, with tears, to forgive him and not kill him; and as a mother entreating the judge with tears, that he may not sentence her son to death.

Likewise did the great saints weep and shed tears before God when they saw one of them fall into sin or slip, that God may be patient with him and may not let him die in his fall, but rather He may open the door of repentance before him to stand up again. Such were the tears of St. Augustine's mother, St. Monica, through which he was born again, but this time not from the fruit of her womb; rather from the fountain of her eyes which did not cease, not even for a day, from shedding tears for his sake. Concerning this St. Ambrose said to her, "It is not possible that the son of these tears should perish."[80] St. Augustine, in his soliloquy to God concerning his mother, says, "But I will not omit anything at all that my soul has brought forth as to that Your handmaid who brought me forth,—in her flesh, that I might be born to this temporal light, and in

---

79 See The Divine Liturgy – Fraction to the Son: O Only-begotten Son.

80 St. Augustine *The Confessions of St. Augustine* 3.XII.21 (NPNF[1] 1).

her heart, that I might be born to life eternal,"[81] and, "I was granted to the faithful and daily tears of my mother, that I should not perish."[82]

Likewise was St. Paesia born from the fountain of tears of St. John the Short,[83] where his tears softened her heart and made her abandon everything, offer the most profound repentance, and go with him to the wilderness. There he saw her spirit ascend to heaven, amidst the angels in a pillar of light. And heaven testified that her repentance was sincere and acceptable more than the repentance of many.

Also when the heart is constricted in an internal struggle of the heart with God, or in an entreaty without audible words, then tears flow spontaneously as a result to this silent struggle of the heart. For when Jesus wept before the tomb of Lazarus, this was not because of the death of Lazarus, for He knew this before His long journey to the tomb, four days prior; neither did He weep for the sake of Mary and Martha, because He knew what He would do for their sakes. Rather, He wept because He was praying in His heart to God the Father, a silent prayer of the heart, indicated by His saying, "Father, I thank You

---

81   St. Augustine *The Confessions of St. Augustine* 9.VIII.17 (NPNF[1] 1).

82   St. Augustine *A Treatise on the Predestination of the Saints* 2.53 (NPNF[1] 5).

83   See *Give Me a Word: The Alphabetical Sayings of the Desert Fathers*, J. Wortley, trans. (Yonkers, NY: SVS Press, 2014), John Colobos 40.

that You have heard Me."[84]

There is an important difference between Mary's tears, whom Jesus saw weeping, and Jesus' tears when He wept. The Greek word "weep" used for the weeping of Mary means crying aloud and wailing, while that used to describe the weeping of Jesus is another Greek word that indicates silent weeping with tears.

As for what the Father heard from His Son Jesus Christ, this no one heard, for it was an inward groaning issuing from the depths and ascending to the highest heights. For this reason, the tears of the Lord Jesus flowed.

We also ought to realize something important, which the Lord brought to our attention; that is, the grace of tears in prayer will not always be the result of a single prayer or according to acuteness of passing feelings. Rather, it is a grace that comes through continuance and perseverance. Therefore, He finished His word, by saying, "And I know that You always hear Me."[85]

And all those who tasted the delight of tears that are born of prayer, do not cease from asking for them persistently and always. Concerning this the marvelous St. Arsenius testifies, who did not at all cease from weeping, until his eyelids withered, and his eyelashes fell off. For tears were his constant,

---

84 John 11:41.

85 John 11:42.

silent praise until he departed this life while his eyelids were wet with tears.

Let us then struggle to make God hear the voices of our hearts at all times. For even if tears do not come in a tangible way, according to the difference of our bodies, they will undoubtedly be counted before God as tears from heart to heart, and they will be written in His book. They will neither dry up nor be erased at all, as is the case with the ordinary, natural tears.

4. Do Prostrations

We also need prostrations and many acts of worship, with which we enter the presence of God. Therefore, we say in the beginning of the Morning Prayer in the Agpeya, "O come, let us worship, let us ask.... O come, let us worship, let us entreat.... O come, let us worship, let us implore Christ our Savior." This is taken from psalm 95: "Oh come, let us worship and bow down; let us kneel before the Lord our Maker."[86] Foremost it is right that we submit to God, bowing before Him through worshiping (serving Him) and prostrations (repentance and return).

This right Paul the Apostle emphasized, as it previously came in the Psalms and Prophets,[87] saying, "For it is written: 'As I live, says the Lord,

---

86   Psalms 95:6.

87   See Psalms 72:9 and Isaiah 45:23.

every knee shall bow to Me, and every tongue shall confess to God.'"[88] Asking and entreating require a bowed and contrite soul, that its entreaty may come before God.

Whoever desires to repent ought to change his course which was inclined toward sin. And prostrations[89] are the expression with which we show God the change of our mind toward Him. And this cannot be fulfilled except through prayer in contrition and through many prostrations in the inner room, far from the eyes of men. Therefore, St. Isaac the Syrian says, "Whoever thinks that there is another way to repentance except prayer is deceived by the demons."[90]

Prostrations then are a bodily expression of the feelings of repentance issuing from a contrite heart. They represent a confession of having fallen and committed sin, and then becoming roused and rising as a resurrection from the earth and death to heaven and eternal life.

Let us, my beloved, remember that during the miracle of the Mokattam Mountain, the mountain would lift up and move from its place with every prostration the people did. And so we can tear down the mountain of bad habits in us and can expel

---

88   Romans 14:11.

89   The Arabic word is *metania*, which comes from the Greek, meaning "change of mind."

90   Cf. *Bostan Al-Rohban* [Paradise of the Monks], Bishop Epiphanius, ed. (Cairo, Egypt: Dar Majalat Marcus, 2014), 415.

sin out. Prostrations, my beloved, also terrify the demons and destroy their plots.

5. Seek the intercessions of the saints

Many people say that there is no direct commandment that says that we ought to pray through the intercessions of the saints. When a person humbles himself, however, feeling that he is a sinner, unworthy of standing before God, he feels that he needs the saints to carry his prayers to God on his behalf. For they are righteous and have boldness before Him. This then is the proof of the contrition of heart and its humility. As the psalm says, "A broken and a contrite heart—these, O God, You will not despise,"[91] and in the Septuagint, it says, "A broken and humbled heart God will not despise."[92] I must live in humility, so that God may not despise me and reject me, feeling in the depth of myself that I am unworthy to stand in prayer before God, humbly seeking the intercession of the saints for me.

The Scripture speaks to us about the intercession of Abraham for the sake of Sodom and Gomorrah, that God may forgive them if there were only ten righteous men among them, and the Lord accepted his intercession.[93] But, unfortunately, there were

---

91   Psalms 51:17.

92   Psalms 50:17 LXX.

93   See Genesis 18:16–33.

only three persons in the entire two cities: Lot and his daughters. Lot's wife left with them indeed, but her heart was still in Sodom. And if the number had reached ten men, God would not have burned the place, in response to Abraham's intercession.

We have also learned about God's acceptance of Moses' intercession for the sake the people, that He may not destroy them after they had worshipped the gold calf,[94] and his intercession for Aaron and Miriam his sister after they sinned against him.[95] We also read of Samuel's intercession for the sin of the people.[96]

And after many years, when the sins of the people were greatly multiplied, the thing which made Jeremiah the prophet weep before God with copious tears, interceding for their sakes, that they may not be taken into captivity, the Lord finally said to him, to give him rest from his much weeping for the sake of the people, "Even if Moses and Samuel stood before Me, My mind would not be favorable toward this people. Cast them out of My sight."[97] This means that God was ready to accept the intercession of Moses and Samuel, who were not alive at that time, except that all the people, who were present at the time of Jeremiah, were unworthy of the acceptance of the intercession of anyone,

94 See Exodus 32:11–14.
95 See Numbers 12:13.
96 See 1 Samuel 7:7–9.
97 Jeremiah 15:1.

58

neither of Moses nor Samuel, the most famous two who successfully interceded for their children. Even Jeremiah himself, the weeping prophet for their sakes, the enormity and multitude of the people's sins prevented his intercession from being heard, where the long-suffering of God reached its pinnacle; therefore, God decided to deliver them, each to his fate, saying, "Such as are for death, to death; and such as are for the sword, to the sword; and such as are for the famine, to the famine; and such as are for the captivity, to the captivity."[98]

Truly, the rejection of Jeremiah's intercession was nothing but mercy for the remainder who survived, whose hearts were still ready for a life in the fear of the Lord and walking in His commandments, like Daniel, the three youths, Nehemiah, Ezra, Tobias, Esther, Susanna, and others of those who remained.

For had they remained in Jerusalem, amidst the painful offenses, they would have suffered the loss of their fear of God and their spiritual fervor, according to the prophecy of Isaiah the prophet, "Unless the LORD of hosts had left to us a very small remnant, we would have become like Sodom, we would have been made like Gomorrah."[99] Their condition was warning of a moral catastrophe like what happened in Sodom and Gomorrah, if God left the new generations to grow and be raised

---

98   Jeremiah 15:2.
99   Isaiah 1:9.

amidst these degenerating transgressions. Therefore, the means for delivering them was the trial and tribulation of the captivity.

Nevertheless, throughout the captivity, God did not abandon this little remnant of the faithful saints, but He was preparing them to be intercessors and stewards before Him, to pray for the rest of the people. For God always loves to intervene to rescue and save His servants in response to the intercession of these saints. We have seen before the captivity how the course of His patience and longsuffering was on those evil kings who sat on the throne of David until the time of the captivity, including for example the evil king Abijam (then his son after him), of whom the Scripture says, "Nevertheless for David's sake the Lord his God gave him a lamp in Jerusalem, by setting up his son after him and by establishing Jerusalem."[100]

David then must have been able to intercede for his seed and descendants. Otherwise, what benefit does the Lord receive from keeping these evil kings as kings and rulers over His people, while He knew that they would not repent? David, definitely, participates with Samuel, Isaiah, Jeremiah, and all the saints, living and departed, in interceding for the people and their kings, in hopes that they may repent and return. It is of the kindness of God—and that He listens—that He would send to them His

---

100 1 Kings 15:4.

prophets, one after another, to warn and counsel them, and to pray for them also.

Or do you now think that those saints, whose intercession we seek, who accept to intercede for us with all love and fear for our salvation, have become intercessors for us only by their departure from this world? I do not think so. They were, however, very fervent intercessors during their lives. Then now they are completing their mission and work more powerfully and to a much greater extent after their departure from this body, where their spirits are now resting in paradise, in the bosoms of Abraham, Isaac, and Jacob, where their acceptable intercessions unite with the intercession of the four incorporeal creatures and the twenty-four priests around the heavenly throne, and the heavenly angels, and they rise before God as an acceptable sweet-smelling aroma, as St. John of the revelation shows us, saying:

> The four living creatures and the twenty-four elders fell down before the Lamb, each having a harp, and golden bowls full of incense, which are the prayers of the saints.[101]

> Then another angel, having a golden censer, came and stood at the altar. He was given much incense, that he should offer it with the prayers of all the saints upon the golden

---

101 Revelation 5:8.

altar which was before the throne. And the smoke of the incense, with the prayers of the saints, ascended before God from the angel's hand.[102]

Do you see, my beloved, that he says, "all the saints," and not some of them only? So who are all these saints? He says about them also:

And I saw thrones, and they sat on them, and judgment was committed to them. Then I saw the souls of those who had been beheaded for their witness to Jesus and for the word of God, who had not worshiped the beast or his image, and had not received his mark on their foreheads or on their hands. And they lived and reigned with Christ for a thousand years.[103]

The Church believes that she is currently living in the reign of the thousand years since the time of the crucifixion.

Lord, I am not worthy to stand before you for prayer, but for the sake of the intercession of the Virgin Mary, St. Mark, St. George, and St. Mina— Lord, hear my prayer, I the sinner.

And you too, my brethren, when you seek the

---

102   Revelation 8:3–4.
103   Revelation 20:4.

intercession of these saints, you ought to learn how to be like them, an intercessor for your brethren, and not their judge.

You ought to always intercede for these among whom you live, and those who care for you and serve you, and also for the ones whom you serve. And you ought to all the more intercede for those in whom you see a weakness or signs of having fallen, for they are in dire need for a faithful intercession for them. And you also ought to intercede for the rulers and those holding a position [of authority], and for sinners and those who have fallen and deviated. Be like Abba Paul the first hermit and Abba Karus and others of the fathers who used to intercede always for the sake of the whole world—and they still do so until now—of whom it was said that through their prayers the Lord sent rain and goodness upon the whole earth.

6

The Result of the Act of Prayer

What happens when a person prays? St. Paul says, "The peace of God, which surpasses all understanding, will guard your hearts and minds through Christ Jesus."[104] This is the Gospel response the Church uses during the holy Great Fast period.

The Lord Christ says, "Peace I leave with you, My peace I give to you; not as the world gives do I give to you."[105] The peace of the world is connected with the gifts of the world. When someone receives something, they are happy with it and smile, but after a while they return to their sadness and disturbance, and they discover that this peace, which they felt, was nothing but a transient and false peace.

---

104   Philippians 4:7.
105   John 14:27.

The important thing is the following: Is the peace of the world capable of giving consolation at the time of tribulation? I do not think so. But let us see how the peace of God surpasses all understanding.

Herod seized James the Apostle and killed him. The day after, he seized Peter and cast him into prison, so that he might kill him as he killed James. Imagine—a person who is imprisoned and who knows that the following day he will be led to be executed! In what state will he be? When one of us has an ordinary case only, they cannot sleep from the intensity of anxiety and from thinking about their case. Peter, however, who enjoyed the peace of God which surpasses all understanding, was asleep—not an ordinary sleep only, but a very deep sleep, to the extent that the angel, when he came to deliver him, struck him on his side, so that he may wake him up, to take him out of prison.[106]

St. Paul and St. Silas, what did they do in prison? "Singing hymns to God."[107] And when the Lord opened the doors of the prison for them, they did not run away. This was so that they may preach to the keeper of the prison and may capture his soul for Christ.

St. Stephen, when he was persecuted, judged and then stoned, the Scripture says concerning him, "And all who sat in the council, looking steadfastly

106 See Acts 12:7.
107 Acts 16:25.

at him, saw his face as the face of an angel."[108] As the face of an angel, meaning wrapped in light, his face and countenance being full of peace.

Likewise the rest of the martyrs at the time of their persecution, like St. Mina, St. Abanoub, St. Demiana, and others, their faces and countenance were full of peace. Why? Because the peace of God, which surpasses all understanding. With this surpassing peace the Holy Spirit overwhelms us, "whom the world cannot receive, because it neither sees Him nor knows Him,"[109] but we know Him, for He dwells with us and is in us since the day we were baptized into Christ.[110]

This does not mean that God gives us all that we want and desire, so that we may enjoy this peace. When we ask something from God, why does He not give it to us? This is certainly because it is not for our benefit. God gave St. Paul the Apostle a thorn in the flesh, and he prayed and said, "Concerning this thing I pleaded with the Lord three times that it might depart from me."[111] Did the thorn leave him after he prayed? No, it did not, but the Lord said to him, "My grace is sufficient for you, for My strength is made perfect in weakness."[112] Therefore, he said, "Therefore most gladly I will rather boast

---

108   Acts 6:15.
109   John 14:17.
110   See ibid.
111   2 Corinthians 12:8.
112   2 Corinthians 12:9.

in my infirmities, that the power of Christ may rest upon me."[113] We see here that weakness and illness were the reason for the success of Paul the Apostle, and were the reason for the power which rested upon him from Christ. And this is the peace of God which surpasses all understanding.

When I pray to God, the result, of which I am absolutely confident, is that God will give me peace. When I pray for someone who is ill, that the Lord may heal them, it is not important that the Lord heals this person who is ill, as He did not heal Paul the Apostle; rather, the important thing is that He will give the person peace.

Therefore, when the three saintly youths prayed, God did not prevent them from being cast into the furnace of fire; rather, He came down to them, to be with them in the midst of the furnace. And when Daniel prayed, God did not prevent him from being thrown into the den of lions; rather, He sent His angel and shut the lions' mouths, so that they did not hurt him. And God was with him and gave him peace.

"The peace of God, which surpasses all understanding, will guard your hearts and minds through Christ Jesus."[114]

When a trial or a difficult problem comes upon one of us, we may perhaps suffer from diabetes or

---

113 Ibid.
114 Philippians 4:7.

high blood pressure, for example; our mind may become troubled and we lose self-control; we may complain and grumble, and our trust in ourselves and in God may be weakened; or perhaps we may become violent in our dealings with others, always losing our temper and losing those around us.

On the complete opposite, however, when a person possesses the peace of God, the peace of God preserves the mind from anxious thinking and preserves the heart also from sin and error, so that the person does not sin against God during the tribulation. Neither will they attempt to run away from it, nor to surrender to it. On the contrary, they accept it courageously, endure it open-heartedly, thank God for its sake, and even benefit from it and obtain its blessings and consolations. They know that, like the three youths, they can see God through it.

Abba Paul [the Simple] says, "He who flees from tribulation flees from God."[115] It is then a meeting with God, in which there are good experiences, and deeper knowledge of Him, and certainty that you will be crowned with consolations and joy. The Lord Christ, during the trial and severe tribulation, "prayed more earnestly,"[116] so the angel of the Lord appeared to Him, to strengthen Him.

---

115 *Bostan Al-Rohban Al-Mowasah, Al-joz' Al-Awal* [The Expanded Paradise of the Monks, Vol. 1]. (Egypt: St. Macarius Monastery, 2006), 222.

116 Luke 22:44.

Likewise does the Christian deal with a tribulation. They pray and pray even more. They pray more earnestly, regardless of the severity of the trial, being confident in their heart that after every cross there must be a resurrection and joy. And not only that, but also an ascension to glory, and peace that has not entered into the heart of man and is beyond description. This is exactly as Paul the Apostle says, "But in everything by prayer and supplication, with thanksgiving, let your requests be made known to God; and the peace of God, which surpasses all understanding, will guard your hearts and minds through Christ Jesus."[117]

---

117 Philippians 4:6–7.

7

Types of Prayer

There are seven main types of prayer, and they may be individual or communal. And they are the following: supplication, crying out during tribulation, prayer of thanksgiving, contemplative prayer, prayer of praise, personal canon prayer, and unceasing prayer.

1. Supplication

We have previously explained how Hannah, Samuel's mother, made her request, and likewise St. Euphemia, St. Mina's mother, and we learned from the explanation of St. Paul the Apostle how our requests are made known before God, until an answer comes. Here we will speak briefly about seven types of supplications. After that we will address the second type of prayer, which is the crying out during tribulation.

First, supplications that are not answered

His Holiness Pope Shenouda III taught us that the answer of a prayer is sometimes that it is not answered, for God knows more than we do what is good for us. And out of His love for us, He does not give us what may harm us or may cause our perdition.

For God either answers immediately, or answers at the appropriate time, or answers by not giving us what we requested. In these circumstances, we remember how Paul the Apostle asked three times for healing from a thorn in his flesh, which caused him pain, but God refused to answer his request, for the sake of his salvation, and He said to him, "My grace is sufficient for you, for My strength is made perfect in weakness."[118] See how great the grace of God is, which has come upon us now! And how strong the power of God is, which is reserved for us at the time of weakness and tribulation!

Second, supplications which are not in agreement with the will of God

We make these supplications, without knowing whether they are in agreement with God's will or not, and through our persistence and continuance in supplication, the Lord reveals to us His will. And at once we are certain that if God had fulfilled [lit.

---

118   2 Corinthians 12:9.

answered] to us these requests, they would have caused us problems and tribulations. Also they were absolutely not the needs we hoped for. Therefore, we ought to thank Him each time, for having not fulfilled these requests.

And perhaps of the examples of these requests is when the Philistines went up to attack David's army once again. So David asked the Lord whether he ought to go up to face the Philistines like the first time, but God gave him the opposite answer and another plan which includes great hardship and toil for him and his army. This is perhaps so that they may not become proud and exalted because of their victory the first time, and the Lord said to David, "You shall not go up; circle around behind them, and come upon them in front of the mulberry trees."[119]

Third, supplications whose time has not come yet

These requests may be in agreement with God's will for us, but God refuses to fulfill [lit. answer] them for us at a particular time. Then He gives them to us at the appropriate time, in which we can truly benefit from them. And finally God's wisdom appears before us, through His delay in answering.

An example of such supplications is Abraham's

---

119 2 Samuel 5:23.

supplication that God may give him offspring. God tarried long for about twenty years, until all the human standards and hopes were destroyed, especially after he was almost a hundred years old, and his wife Sarah was ninety years old, and she had "passed the age of childbearing,"[120] and Sarah's womb was dead.[121]

Also Joseph the righteous, he used to groan under the heavy yoke of slavery, feeling his brothers' injustice against him. And he certainly used to ask God to save him from these chains and this injustice. Nevertheless, what is worse took place: he was thrown into prison for several years, and the injustice was multiplied even more against him, despite his innocence. Also when he met with Pharaoh's butler and baker in prison, and when God revealed to him the interpretation of their dreams, he supposed that God had finally managed the issue of his release, revealing his innocence, as evidenced by him asking Pharaoh's butler to remember him when he appears before Pharaoh. That is to say, he had a pressing desire to be released. This, however, was not the time for fulfillment [i.e. answering] as he had expected, but he continued in prison for a longer time. And when the appointed time from the Lord came, in the fullness of its time, the fulfillment to his request did not come alone, but came with it great blessings, which came neither to his mind

---

120 Genesis 18:11.

121 See Romans 4:19.

nor to the mind of anyone else. And he became the second man in the kingdom after Pharaoh, and this would not have happened if he had gone out at the time when the king's butler went out.

Likewise also is the supplication of Zacharias and Elizabeth, that God may give them offspring, where God delayed for long to answer their supplication. Then at the appointed time, God gave them St. John the Baptist, the greatest of those born of women,[122] the forerunner, who prepared the way before Christ.[123]

Fourth, improper supplications

Not only are these requests the ones we ask in ignorance and lack of knowledge, but they are also not in agreement with the commandments of God and the teachings of the Holy Scriptures. For example, someone might ask God to take vengeance for him on someone else who has wronged him, or a poor person might ask God to make him rich in money, or a rich person might ask to have increase in wealth, authority, and status, or in general the purpose behind it is worldly or sensual, and not for the sake of the kingdom of God and His righteousness, nor for the glory of His holy name. And our teacher James the Apostle explained it to us in his epistle, saying, "You ask and do not receive,

---

122 See Luke 7:28.
123 See Luke 1:13–18.

because you ask amiss, that you may spend it on your pleasures."[124]

Those, who are immature[125] in the spiritual life and have not yet entered into the early stages of the fitting relationship with God, often fall into these. Such supplications require repentance and confession. And it is not unlikely that those advanced spiritually fall into these, either because they have become proud, or because of indifference[126] or weakness in the spiritual relationship, or even during falling and straying away from God because of sin.

Jonah the prophet is an example of this, who was delivered from the belly of the fish and fulfilled his evangelical mission, for the sake of which God sent him. Then after he learned that God had accepted the repentance of the people of Nineveh and that He had gone back on the resolute punishment which He was about to bring down upon the city, he became angry and exceedingly displeased because of this. And he asked God, saying, "'Therefore now, O Lord, please take my life from me, for it is better for me to die than to live!' Then the Lord said, 'Is it right for you to be angry?'"[127]

And of course God did not fulfill [or answer]

---

124 James 4:3.

125 Literally: babes.

126 Literally: coldness.

127 Jonah 4:3–4.

this supplication for him, but rather He gently guided him to realize the enormity of his error.

Fifth, supplications that are inspired by the Holy Spirit

These are requests which the Holy Spirit places in the sons of God, the saints, so they ask them at a particular time. Then God answers them for them, based on His wisdom and His unsearchable economy.

An example of this is Elijah's supplication to stop the rain, then his supplication that it may rain again after three years and six months. The power of the Spirit made him, while still unknown as a great prophet in Israel, stand with all courage before Ahab the king, saying, "As the Lord God of Israel lives, before whom I stand, there shall not be dew nor rain these years, except at my word."[128]

This great prophet always felt, all the days of his life, that he was standing before the Lord, and his famous phrase became tightly associated with him: "As the Lord God of Israel lives, before whom I stand." From him his disciple Elisha learned it and repeated it also.[129] As Elijah always felt that he was standing in the presence of the Lord while on earth, so he became worthy to stand in the presence of the

---

128   1 Kings 17:1.
129   2 Kings 5:16.

Lord in heaven, after a chariot of fire took him to heaven, that he may remain alive in the body until the time comes for the fulfillment of his mission with Enoch the righteous, as we read in the Book of Revelation.

I wish that we learned the fear of being before the Lord all the days of our lives on earth, from Elijah, Elisha, and the disciples, so that the supplications we make may be inspired by the Holy Spirit, to be worthy of standing before Him in His kingdom, forever.

Another example is the supplication Daniel made for the sake of ending the people's captivity and their return to Jerusalem. Daniel was a first-rate man of prayer. For despite the fact that his ever-increasing responsibilities as the second man in the empire were vast, which included most of the old world at that time, this did not prevent him from persisting daily in prayer, kneeling down, and thanksgiving, at least three times per day.[130] We all know that for this reason he was cast into the lions' den twice.[131] In the ninth chapter of the Book of Daniel, we sense the fervor of his prayer for his people, and his confession of his sins and the sins of his people:

O Lord, according to all Your righteousness,

---

130 Daniel 6:10.
131 The second time appears in the Deuterocanonical books.

I pray, let Your anger and Your fury be turned away from Your city Jerusalem, Your holy mountain; because for our sins, and for the iniquities of our fathers, Jerusalem and Your people are a reproach to all those around us. Now therefore, our God, hear the prayer of Your servant, and his supplications, and for the Lord's sake cause Your face to shine on Your sanctuary, which is desolate. O my God, incline Your ear and hear; open Your eyes and see our desolations, and the city which is called by Your name; for we do not present our supplications before You because of our righteous deeds, but because of Your great mercies. O Lord, hear! O Lord, forgive! O Lord, listen and act! Do not delay for Your own sake, my God, for Your city and Your people are called by Your name.[132]

We sense persistence and self-abasement in the prayer of Daniel and his supplication which was inspired by the Spirit, and the repeated calling on the Lord several times, saying, "O Lord.... O Lord, hear! O Lord, forgive! O Lord, listen and act!"—all this was done with great humility and poverty, while covering himself with sackcloth and ashes,[133] as the custom was in these days to express humility and self-abasement before God. Therefore,

---

132 Daniel 9:16–19.

133 See Daniel 9:3.

Archangel Gabriel came and made known to him that heaven calls him "greatly beloved," then he explained to him important details concerning the response [or answer] to his prayers and concerning other mysteries which had not come into his mind regarding the fate of the entire human race. Before the revelation of a prophecy and divine mysteries, always come prayer and supplication with humility and contrition.

Nehemiah's supplication for the building of the wall of Jerusalem is another example. Nehemiah followed in the footsteps of Elijah, Jeremiah, and Daniel, beginning his prayers by confessing the sins of all his people and the fathers of his people which were the cause of the captivity. He is as though the one responsible for the sins before the Lord and is a participant in them. Then he confessed his own sins also, his and his father's house's, saying in his prayer, "Please let Your ear be attentive and Your eyes open, that You may hear the prayer of Your servant which I pray before You now, day and night, for the children of Israel Your servants, and confess the sins of the children of Israel which we have sinned against You. Both my father's house and I have sinned."[134] The Lord supported his prayers through Haggai the prophet, not only by the success and completion of building the wall, but also by the completion of building the temple and the entire city.

---

134   Nehemiah 1:6.

Yet another example is the supplication of Paul to preach the gospel in Rome. The Scripture says, "When these things were accomplished, Paul purposed in the Spirit, when he had passed through Macedonia and Achaia, to go to Jerusalem, saying, 'After I have been there, I must also see Rome.'"[135] And we see that awhile after this how the Lord approves his supplication when He appeared to him in prison in Jerusalem, saying, "Be of good cheer, Paul; for as you have testified for Me in Jerusalem, so you must also bear witness at Rome."[136]

The blessing of the fulfillment [or answering] of most of these supplications is not only limited to those who requested them, but it includes also the rest of the people or many others. And it is not far from you that the Holy Spirit place a supplication in you, or supplications inspired by Him, that you may request them before Him with humility and poverty.

In the history of the Church and the life accounts of the fathers, we find many timeless, living examples of such supplications: for example, the supplication of Pope Peter the holy martyr for the ending of the era of martyrdom; and the supplication of Abba Paul the first hermit, that God may raise the water of the Nile in its due time, so that the country may not suffer from famine or drought; and the supplication

---

135 Acts 19:21.
136 Acts 23:11.

of Abba Macarius the Great for the sake of the continuation of monasticism in Scetis.

Sixth, supplications for others

It is an aspect of supplications inspired by the Holy Spirit, which are considered the most sublime kind of supplications and most pleasing to the heart of God. In this kind of prayer, a person goes out of the sphere of himself and his needs, and is occupied by the needs and requests of others. By this he expresses his practical and true love for them, where there is no place, for example, for boasting before someone or flattering them.

The New Testament alone contains more than fifty commandments urging us to care for one another as an expression of the evangelical love. For example, "You also ought to wash one another's feet,"[137] "have peace with one another,"[138] and, "that you love one another."[139] But the most impactful and comprehensive are the prayer and supplication for one another, concerning which St. James the Apostle says in his epistle, "Pray for one another, that you may be healed. The effective, fervent prayer of a righteous man avails much."[140] This is supported by what St. Paul the Apostle asked of his disciple

---

137 John 13:14.

138 Mark 9:50.

139 John 13:34 and John 15:12.

140 James 5:16.

Timothy, giving it priority over everything else: "Therefore I exhort first of all that supplications, prayers, intercessions, and giving of thanks be made for all men."[141]

In the past, when the people refused for Samuel the prophet to be a judge over them, and asked for a king who would go out and come in before them like the rest of the nations, they then realized the enormity of their sin and apologized to him, asking for his prayers for their sakes that they may not die. He answered them, saying, "Moreover, as for me, far be it from me that I should sin against the LORD in ceasing to pray for you."[142] That is, Samuel the prophet considered the mere ceasing from praying for all the people a sin counted against him, no matter how much they reject him and sin and commit offense against him and against the authority of the priesthood and of his being a judge appointed by God.

Also David the prophet in his psalms, besides his cries because of his tribulations and the rising of his enemies against him, we find that in the end, he is overcome by the spirit of supplication and prayer for the sake of Israel and all the people, especially the awaited salvation of us all, through the coming of the Lord Jesus Christ and His incarnation.

And a person grows in true love, day by day,

141 1 Timothy 2:1.
142 1 Samuel 12:23.

as the sphere of those he prays and supplicates for expands, that he may go out of the sphere of his relatives, acquaintances, and friends, that it may extend to all the members of his church, all those living in his community and city, to include also all those who mistreat him, persecute him, or insult and wrong him, according to the commandment of our good Savior; but even that it may extend to his entire generation, and the whole world and creation, as the saints did, of whom it was said, "of whom the world was not worthy,"[143] such saints as Abba Paul the first hermit, Abba Karus, Abba Pishoy the beloved of our good Savior, Abba Nopher the anchorite, St. Anna-Simone the queen of the beasts, and others, who did not cease from praying and supplicating for the salvation of the world and deliverance of men.

And so are the spirits of the prophets and saints always occupied with prayer for the sake of all, and the love of all, and the salvation of all.

And perhaps the greatest example, from which we may learn this prayer, which is full of blessing and grace, is the intercessional prayer which the Lord Christ offered for His disciples and for us who have believed through their word and preaching: "I do not pray for these alone, but also for those who will believe in Me through their word."[144]

This was in the seventeenth chapter of the Gospel

---

143 Hebrews 11:38.

144 John 17:20.

of St. John, which is considered the greatest pearl of the prayers present in the Holy Scriptures. The Church gives it, with the three preceding chapters, the title "The Gospel of the Paraclete," that is the Comforter. It is a wonderful and profound prayer, in which the Lord Christ asks of His good Father that we all be one in Him and in His Father, enjoying what He has of eternal glory, saying:

> Holy Father, keep through Your name those whom You have given Me, that they may be one as We are.... that they all may be one, as You, Father, are in Me, and I in You; that they also may be one in Us.... And the glory which You gave Me I have given them, that they may be one just as We are one.... Father, I desire that they also whom You gave Me may be with Me where I am, that they may behold My glory which You have given Me. [145]

He also asks for them the perfection of eternal love: "That the love with which You loved Me may be in them, and I in them." [146] And He asks for constant, true joy: "These things I speak in the world, that they may have My joy fulfilled in themselves." [147] He also asks for them deliverance from Satan and his

---

145 John 17:11, 21–22, 24.
146 John 17:26.
147 John 17:13.

destructive plots and snares, throughout their time on earth: "I do not pray that You should take them out of the world, but that You should keep them from the evil one."[148] Likewise He asks for them constant holiness, as He Himself is pure and holy: "Sanctify them by Your truth. Your word is truth.... And for their sakes I sanctify Myself, that they also may be sanctified by the truth."[149]

I wonder if there is something greater than that, that we ask that someone else may be in the Father and the Son and the Holy Spirit, and a partaker of the glory of the Trinity, enjoying the eternal joy which is indescribable, always preserved from the evil one and his evil deeds, and that he may be perfect in the constant divine love, and holy in the Truth who is Jesus Christ, the true God?

All these are eternal supplications, which we can train ourselves to pray with, and which we can pray for the sake of others.

Seventh, supplication for the quick Second Coming of the Lord

This is a very high and sublime kind of supplication, yet the Church taught us to request it always, and we express this supplication at the end of the Orthodox Creed, saying, "And we look for the resurrection of

---

148 John 17:15.
149 John 17:17, 19.

the dead, and the life of the age to come. Amen." And because of the great importance of this supplication and because of the intensity of the longing of the Church for its fulfillment, this phrase in particular is chanted with a special loud tune in church, unlike the way the rest of the Creed is recited.

St. Peter the Apostle advises us to make this supplication frequently, saying, "Looking for and hastening the coming of the day of God, because of which the heavens will be dissolved, being on fire, and the elements will melt with fervent heat."[150]

It is the supplication of the true believers who are ready. It is the supplication of the five wise virgins, who are waiting for their bridegroom. It is the supplication of the faithful servants who are watching, awaiting the coming of the Lord of the house. It is the supplication of the faithful steward, whom his master made ruler over all that he had. It is the supplication of all those who are trading with the talents and multiplying them with labor and diligence. It is the supplication of every soul who is delighting in divine love, who hides from sight, to entreat her loved One.

It is the supplication of the conclusion of the word of God in the Holy Scripture, requesting it with the longing and yearning of the bride the Church, and every human soul who loves her Bridegroom and longs for Him, saying, "Amen. Even so, come,

---

150   2 Peter 3:12.

Lord Jesus!"[151]

A model for an acceptable supplication

Let us suppose that you want God to save you from the habit of being quick-tempered. If you have read influential books by the most famous psychologists, and have made use of unfailing exercises, and have strengthened your determination to the uttermost, yet have not asked for the grace and help of God, you will certainly fail. Nevertheless, if you abide by the following steps, the Lord, through His grace, will crown your struggle with success.

1. When you wake up early in the morning, thank God, then ask Him, saying, "I beseech You, Lord, You who have granted the Manna to the children of Israel day by day, grant that I may overcome the sin of anger on this holy day." You ought to realize, however, that every gift or virtue you ask for from God, as we have indicated, requires from you struggle, persistence, and faith.

2. Throughout your day, repeat the following phrase, as much as you can: "My Lord Jesus Christ, the Son of God, save me from the sin of anger." To avoid forgetting, especially in the beginning, you may write it on a small piece of paper and stick it in front of you in the places where you may be, at work, at home, and in the car. If you are embarrassed

---

151 Revelation 22:20.

for it to be seen by those around you—despite their knowledge of your temperance—you may place it in your personal drawer, so that you may see it and remember whenever you open the drawer. Or it may be better for you to make a notification with a reminder, in your schedule on your phone; or you may do this and that, yet the important thing is that you should know the suitable method by which you may remember.

3. Besides that, if you struggle according to the rules, you may seek the help of the exercises indicated by psychologists, especially those in the Christian counseling books. There are many methods available, and you can choose the one that fits your personality and circumstances, and here is one of the known methods which brings quick and effective results.

Set aside a particular amount of money, according to your ability; let us say $3, for example. When you suddenly become agitated and angry, as soon as you realize this, kindly excuse yourself from the people before whom you became angry, and quietly retreat and go outside. And the first person you meet, whom you sense to be poor and in need, give him this amount at once. And if you were truly serious, having left the house at two in the morning, on a very cold day, after a fit of anger with your spouse for example, and finding nobody in need, and desiring to return home quickly, then give the amount to the closest person you meet, even if you are sure that he is not in need. Also, you should be prepared, before doing so, to be insulted by the person because of this action of yours. Pray in your heart that you will endure it for the sake of Christ, or instead, do it in a polite and friendly way; that is, flatter the person with a word or two, then ask him to take the money while he is on good terms with you. And if he asks you for the reason, do not hide the matter from him, but explain to him that this is in exchange for a bad habit you are trying to eliminate. And perhaps through this you will witness to Christ before him, and to the life of virtue and the Christian struggle. The Lord Christ may have sent him to you specifically, so that you may participate in his salvation. But do not postpone this or say for example, "I will wait until I go to church and will put it in the box." If you become weak and fall into two or three fits of anger without doing so, then you must rid yourself of their account as soon as possible, giving it to the first person you meet. Otherwise, the money of injustice will be in your pocket, and a proof of failure.

When you use this exercise with prayer and through the grace of our Lord, you will notice in your bank statement that the amount that came out of your pocket in the second month, for example, was much less than that in the first month, and so you will arrive at the day, in which you will say to yourself, through the grace of Christ, "Controlling my nerves and not getting angry are much easier than going out of the house at a late or early hour, to look for someone to give him the $3." And so a month passes after another without you falling into this sin and without having to pay anything because of it.

4. Whether you use this exercise or that, you must sit with yourself every day and count how many times you became angry. If a day passes without becoming angry or agitated, stand up at once and offer a short thanksgiving prayer to God, who made you pass through the entire day without anger. But if you had become angry, stand up too and offer a prayer, apologizing and repenting to God, asking for His help in your struggle the following day. Also put it in your heart that you must offer an apology to the one you were angry at. The issue is not who was at fault or the cause, but your issue is that you committed the sin of anger against God and your neighbor. And the day will come in which the Lord will crown your struggle, not only with success, but also with another virtue as a gift and congratulation from Him, or perhaps much more than you may imagine.

So everyone of us may apply the same steps on any weakness we suffer from in our lives, smoking for example, or the secret habit, or stealing, or lying, or pornography, or any kind of addiction or other sins. As for the perfect, they may apply it on the virtues which they have not done, for example not going to Liturgy, or service, or visitation, or negligence in your spiritual canon or helping someone in need. For the Holy Spirit, as He convicts us of sin, also convicts us of the righteousness and goodness which we did not do.

2. Crying out during tribulation

Every one of us must go through a tribulation, or even several tribulations at the same time. The Lord Christ told us in His teaching that these tribulations would not be strange to us, and He Himself went through many tribulations.

He made Himself poor while He is rich, and He lived among us, having forsaken His glory. He came as a stranger and poor, and had nowhere to lay His head. He went through the temptations of Satan, so that He may give us victory. He was patient with those who said that He had a demon and was mad. He was persecuted by the people of His own country, and once they nearly threw Him down over the cliff, and at another time they were near to stoning Him. Some cities drove Him out, and others did not allow Him to enter. He struggled in profound prayers, full of sorrow and bitterness, to the extent that His sweat became like drops of blood. One of the closest of His loved ones betrayed Him and delivered Him to those who killed Him. His loved ones abandoned Him and ran away from Him. He went through the winepress of sufferings alone, and He endured mocking, nakedness, humiliation, spitting, being struck with the palm of the hand, scourging, beating, crucifixion, drinking sour wine on the cross, and finally death.

But before dying, He commanded us that we should not be troubled or be afraid, nor that we should lose our peace and our faith in Him, if we also pass through tribulations and trials, saying, "These things I have spoken to you, that in Me you may have peace. In the world you will have tribulation; but be of good cheer, I have overcome the world."[152]

At first glance, the meaning of this verse—the intellectual, rational meaning—seems to be that as though you were approaching a very difficult exam, and someone, who had passed this exam before you, would come to you, saying, "This exam is very difficult, but do not worry because I have passed it." Of course, you would say to him, "Your success concerns you only, for what benefit do I get from your own success?"

Through my union with Christ—this is the right understanding of the verse; therefore, the victory is not His alone, but we are victorious over sin, trial, and tribulation, through Christ. While I am united with Christ, I can defeat sin, and also pass through the tribulation and hardship, successfully.

He was not satisfied by assuring our hearts that He would give us the victory, so long as we abide in Him, but St. Paul also explained to us, saying,

152 John 16:33.

"No temptation has overtaken you except such as is common to man; but God is faithful, who will not allow you to be tempted beyond what you are able, but with the temptation will also make the way of escape, that you may be able to bear it."[153]

Through this promise, you would not lose your faith, and your patience would not become weak, and your trust would not waver—neither because of the severity of the tribulation, nor because of the length of its duration. Rather, continue crying out to God in your tribulation, as the psalmist cried out, saying, "In my distress I called upon the LORD, and cried out to my God; He heard my voice from His temple, and my cry entered His ears."[154]

"Though an army may encamp against me, my heart shall not fear; though war may rise against me, in this I will be confident."[155] Christ placed in you all the capabilities of facing a tribulation, and nothing at all can hurt you; therefore, you can confidently say, "I can do all things through Christ who strengthens me."[156]

The abundance of crying out to God in prayer, in the Book of the Psalms specifically, is nothing but an indication of the tribulations and bitter trials which the saintly men of God will go through, at

---

153 1 Corinthians 10:13.

154 2 Samuel 22:7. Also cf. Psalms 18:6.

155 Psalms 27:3.

156 Philippians 4:13.

various times and throughout all generations. All the saintly men of God, the accounts of whose lives we heard, faced their trials and tribulations by prayer and crying out to God, and with joy and consolation at the same time.

The abundance of tribulations and sorrows is what made David the psalmist of Israel. For rather than leading him to depression and sadness, they made him cry out to God, in prayers and praises, resulting in his eventual consolation. This we saw in his psalms and at the end of his life. And so many of the saintly men of God walked in his footsteps. But those who do not find anyone to cry out to in their tribulations and hardships, suffer depression and psychological illnesses, and they live with no consolation.

The reason behind our Lord Jesus Christ's coming as a poor person and a stranger, having "nowhere to lay His head,"[157] being "despised and rejected by men, a Man of sorrows and acquainted with grief,"[158] is so that the least of men in the community may be able to unite with Him and may find hope in Him, without suffering from low self-esteem; and through this union and hope, he can triumph and endure, and even accept thankfully, imitating his Savior and sharing with Him, thereby finding his consolation and joy.

---

157 Matthew 8:20.
158 Isaiah 53:3.

Therefore, the time of tribulation is the golden time for prayer, in which we offer our most profound prayers, full of reverence and contrition. And I hope that we still remember our previous discussion about the benefits of tribulations and trials, and the glory we may acquire through them in the kingdom of God, and even in our present life itself.

3. The Prayer of Thanksgiving

St. Isaac the Syrian says, "Nor does any gift remain without addition, save that which is received without thanksgiving."[159]

David the prophet was accustomed to thanking God in the psalms, even before his request was answered, thanking Him at the same time he was presenting his request, confident that it would be answered. Then he would continue in thanksgiving until the answer actually came, for faith and submission to the will of God were distinguishing features in David's personality and life, not to mention the exceeding thanksgiving which he usually offered after his request was answered.

When the Lord Christ healed the ten men suffering from leprosy, which is deadly and unclean, Jesus commanded them to go and show themselves to the priests, so that the priests may confirm their

---

159 *The Ascetical Homilies of Saint Isaac the Syrian.* (Boston, MA: Holy Transfiguration Monastery, 2011), 120.

healing:

> And one of them, when he saw that he was healed, returned, and with a loud voice glorified God, and fell down on his face at His feet, giving Him thanks. And he was a Samaritan. So Jesus answered and said, "Were there not ten cleansed? But where are the nine? Were there not any found who returned to give glory to God except this foreigner?" And He said to him, "Arise, go your way. Your faith has made you well."[160]

Do you see how the prayer of thanksgiving is capable of saving?

The prayer of thanksgiving is the proof of faith. Therefore, as we said when we spoke about thanksgiving, the Church has arranged to start all her prayers with the prayer of thanksgiving. For our giving of thanks always, as Paul the Apostle says, reflects the state of faith which we are always living, for we never lose our faith at any moment, no matter what conditions and changes we experience.

Unfortunately, we afflict and humble ourselves during our supplications for the things we need, and even more during the prayers we offer when we are experiencing tribulations and trials, but we often completely forget the prayer of thanksgiving

---

160 Luke 17:15–19.

which issues from the heart. This is the case either because of our rejoicing in, and preoccupation with, the gift of God which we had asked for, or because of our rejoicing and preoccupation with the joy of coming out of the tribulation and trial. Even when we remember to thank God first, this is not done with the same fervent prayers which we offered when we were in the state of supplication or in the tribulations and trials.

The Samaritan came back to glorify God "with a loud voice," and not only that, but he also "fell down on his face at His feet, giving Him thanks." Is it not possible for us to offer prayers of thanksgiving in this manner?

4. Contemplative Prayer or Meditations

Contemplative prayer is the prayer of personal retreat, the time of fellowship with God. It is a prayer from the heart, in which the person requests nothing, neither for himself nor for others. It is a prayer in which a person freely expresses whatever is in his heart to God, a prayer in which a person surrenders his feelings to the Holy Spirit, leaving Him to bring out of His inner treasure whatever He desires, old and new. It is an entreaty between an ardent lover, the bride, and her heavenly Bridegroom, where she sees Him with the eyes of her heart in all things surrounding her. Such a prayer gives you clarity of soul, inner rest, and profound spiritual consolation, to the one who prays it and experiences it through much fellowship and repetition.

We have many examples of contemplative prayer in the Holy Scriptures, especially in the Book of Psalms. David the prophet specifically enjoys high sensitivity and possesses fervent feelings toward God, letting no important occasion pass without coming out of it with a beautiful meditation, with which he glorified God and expressed the intensity of his love for Him. For example, if he saw a clear sky and beautiful, sunny weather, he would hurry and compose a psalm, saying, "The heavens declare the glory of God; and the firmament shows His handiwork.... In them He has set a tabernacle for the sun.... Its rising is from one end of heaven."[161]

And during a moonlit night, with the sky adorned with numerous stars, he takes advantage of the sight in a beautiful meditation, saying, "When I consider Your heavens, the work of Your fingers, the moon and the stars, which You have ordained,"[162] with this he moves to the brightness of the glory and dominion which God gave man, saying, "What is man that You are mindful of him, and the son of man that You visit him?... You have made him to have dominion over the works of Your hands; You have put all things under his feet, all sheep and oxen—even the beasts of the field, the birds of the

---

161 Psalms 19:1, 4, 6.

162 Psalms 8:3.

air, and the fish of the sea that pass through the paths of the seas."[163]

And when he encountered an intense thunderstorm with lightnings, we would find him write, saying, "Give unto the LORD, O you mighty ones, give unto the LORD glory and strength.... Worship the LORD in the beauty of holiness. The voice of the LORD is over the waters.... The voice of the LORD breaks the cedars.... The voice of the LORD divides the flames of fire. The voice of the LORD shakes the wilderness.... The LORD sat enthroned at the Flood."[164]

During his work as a shepherd of the sheep, he recorded for us a psalm which is considered one of the most wonderful symphonies in the history of humankind. He switched the roles: rather than it being between himself and his sheep he was tending, he gave the Lord the role of the shepherd who was caring for him, where he likened his soul to a meek lamb in the arm of the Lord, saying:

> The LORD is my shepherd; I shall not want. He makes me to lie down in green pastures; He leads me beside the still waters. He restores my soul; He leads me in the paths of righteousness for His name's sake. Yea, though I walk through the valley of the

---

163 Psalms 8:4, 6–8.
164 Psalms 29:1–3, 5, 7–8, 10.

99

shadow of death, I will fear no evil; for You are with me; Your rod and Your staff, they comfort me.[165]

Then he walks among the high mountains and testifies to the Lord his God and to His greatness, saying, "Who established the mountains by His strength, being clothed with power."[166] He considers the mountains and their establishment an indication of God's power, of spiritual height, and of the Lord's coming upon them; for he says in another psalm, "I will lift up my eyes to the hills—from whence comes my help?"[167] And when he encounters a raging sea, he assures us that the Lord is the One controlling it, saying, "You who still the noise of the seas, the noise of their waves."[168]

Among the rest of his psalms, he placed musical pauses for meditation, which he expressed by the word "Selah," a Hebrew word meaning suspension; or by the word "meditation,"[169] to give opportunity for the human mind to digest the meanings of the words and to store them in his heart, then he is lifted up to heaven, before moving to the next paragraph and the consequent topic; or he may say at the end, "Alleluia," meaning, "rejoice and be joyful in the

---

165 Psalms 23:1–4.

166 Psalms 65:6.

167 Psalms 121:1.

168 Psalms 65:7.

169 Psalms 9:16. This is how it appears in NKJV.

Lord."

David also spoke of the various elements of nature in his meditations, like the stars and constellations, snow and ice, wind and frost, pastures and valleys, fire and heat, darkness and ashes, springs and rivers, trees and grass; and the angels, and the rest of the living creatures like, the lions, serpents, eagles, crows, deer, horses, worms and creeping things.

He meditated at all times: during the tribulations and after they were relieved, during the times of war and the times of peace, at the victory and at the defeat and loss. He even meditated on the inanimate objects and inventions, for God is the One who granted man the wisdom to make them all.

And if we meditated on the prophecies of most of the prophets who came after David, we would find that they walked in his footsteps, especially Isaiah, Jeremiah, Daniel, and Ezekiel.

Therefore, we can learn from the school of David and the other prophets how to meditate on the glory of God and His great works which He did with us, from the time of our birth, in every day of our lives, and even before we were born, until we return to our heavenly country and abide therein forever. Meditation on nature and the creation and the circumstances and changes which God arranges around us, is considered synonymous with the meditation on the Holy Scriptures and the word of God. And of course, the virtue of meditation, like all the other virtues and gifts, is not given except by struggling, perseverance, and repetition. And this is the virtue in which man's inward reception device becomes ready to receive the Holy Spirit's signals and secret inspirations. And we can nearly say that the spiritual man, in his meditations [or contemplations], hears and understands more than what he himself expresses through his being and abilities. And if it is not our intention to struggle to acquire this virtue—or if we are not able to—then at least we should read the meditations of others, of the saints and the honorable men of God, so that perhaps we may share with them in the same blessing and the same consolation which God granted them during their meditations.

The extremely advanced stage of this prayer is a special gift which the Holy Spirit gives to whomever He desires, according to the divine wisdom and purpose for the sake of edification. The fathers call this gift "*theoria*," a Greek word meaning "divine vision," in which the inner eyes of man are opened, to see visions and special mysteries of the divine glory, in different ways according to the degree and endurance of each person.

Of the most famous people in the New Testament who received this lofty gift is St. John the Beloved, who wrote the Book of Revelation. This occurred at the time when he was praying on the Lord's Day (Sunday) on the island of Patmos, where he was exiled because of his preaching.[170] Another one is St. Paul the Apostle, who ascended in the spirit to the third heaven, and "he was caught up into Paradise and heard inexpressible words, which it is not lawful for a man to utter."[171]

Perhaps most of us know the story of Abba John the Short with the camel-driver, who came to take the baskets, the work of his hands from him, to sell them for him. And he kept several times asking him to bring them out to him, but whenever Abba John went inside to bring them, the Spirit would take his mind captive in divine vision, so he would completely forget that the camel-driver was waiting outside his cell. Then the camel-driver would again ask for the baskets. And in an attempt to remember, and not forget, he kept repeating, saying to himself, "Baskets—camel; baskets—camel."[172] But in the end, being wearied of him, he took the camel-driver by the hand and showed him where the baskets were, saying to him, "If it is baskets you want, take [some] and go your way; I do not have the time."[173]

Abba John has written a direction to whoever desires to struggle to attain this high degree of prayer:

170　See Revelation 1.

171　2 Corinthians 12:4.

172　*Give Me a Word: The Alphabetical Sayings of the Desert Fathers*, J. Wortley, trans. (Yonkers, NY: SVS Press, 2014), John Colobos 31.

173　Ibid., John Colobos 30.

If you stand for prayer before God, strive to collect your mind and to cast away from you the thoughts that distract the mind. Place before yourself the honor of God, and purify the motions of your soul from evil thoughts. If you sense grace, persevere and do not slacken. For if God saw your patience, He would let His grace dwell in you quickly, and your mind will be strengthened and burn with fervor, and the thoughts of your heart will shine, and the feelings of astonishment at the greatness of God may well up in you, these which come from many supplications and a pure mind. For just as sweet incense is not placed in a rotten vessel, so does God not manifest His greatness in an evil mind.[174]

In *The Paradise of the Holy Fathers*, we can read numerous stories of many fathers who received this lofty gift, and their disciples recorded only what they coincidentally learned of the elders' trance states and divine visions.

The individual character prevails in this kind of prayer. The fathers have advised that it is necessary for a person to write his meditations, keeping them in his personal journal for himself alone; for it is possible for the person to go back and transform

---

174 *Bostan Al-Rohban Al-Mowasah, Al-joz' Al-Awal* [The Expanded Paradise of the Monks, Vol. 1]. (Egypt: St. Macarius Monastery, 2006), 548.

these meditations into another kind of prayer, that is, praise, exactly like what we do with the psalms of David. He did likewise, by introducing them into the rituals of communal worship in the tabernacle of meeting before the temple was built, and this was through the direction and guidance of the Holy Spirit. Then they were moved and became fundamental to the worship in the temple of Solomon. And this is what our Orthodox Church follows until now in her beautiful rites, and she is devoted to it in almost all her liturgical worship and prayers.

5. The Prayer of Praise

This is absolutely the loftiest and deepest kind of prayers, and the most sublime and holiest, in which the one praying does not request anything, personal or communal. The only purpose rather is the glorification of the name of God, confessing Him and His grace and gifts, and singing His greatness, wisdom, and power. By this holy prayer, we bless our God and exalt Him above all.[175] St. Paul the Apostle commanded us concerning this, considering it as a sacrifice of love we offer to God, "Therefore by Him[176] let us continually offer the sacrifice of praise to God, that is, the fruit of our lips, giving thanks

---

175 See the refrain of the Third Canticle in Midnight Praises.

176 That is, by Christ Jesus.

to His name."[177] And his saying "continually" means as much as possible or according to our ability, at all times.

For this reason the Church has arranged the daily psalmody, dividing it over the seven days of the week. And monastics are most careful about observing it in monasteries, offering it as a firstfruit of their day, giving up the time of the pinnacle of sleep, to offer it to the Lord as the most precious of what they have, as a sacrifice of love confessing His name.

The Lord Jesus Himself participated with His disciples in praising, after He instituted the Mystery of the Eucharist for us on the night of His passion: "And when they had sung a hymn, they went out to the Mount of Olives."[178] For this reason also the Church arranged that the psalm of praise (psalm 150) be sung during the distribution of the Mysteries, for there is no greater joy and gladness than the union with the Lord Jesus by partaking of His Body and Blood.

Praising is an expression of our love for God, and it is the everlasting act which we will perform in eternity as a spontaneous reaction, out of the greatness and awe of what we will know and see of the glory of the Lord, which surpasses understanding.

The prayer of praise is a source of joy, where the

---

177 Hebrews 13:15.
178 Matthew 26:30 and Mark 14:26.

one offering it forgets his worries, problems, and all the world around him, and he only pays attention to the glorification of the name of the Lord. Therefore, the distinguishing feature of this prayer is joy, and so the psalmist cries out, saying, "Serve the LORD with gladness; come before His presence with singing.... Enter into His gates with thanksgiving, and into His courts with praise. Be thankful to Him, and bless His name."[179]

And when I praise, give thanks, and bless the Lord with singing and psalm, then, "May my meditation be sweet to Him; I will be glad in the LORD."[180] For this reason, joy is abundantly multiplied after the prayer of praise, and I will inevitably obtain consolation and largeness of heart. For this prayer is considered the main source of joy and true peace.

Let us then make the prayer of praise one of the main features of our prayers which we offer to God, and let us not delay or be negligent in them, regardless of our preoccupations and works. "My mouth shall speak the praise of the LORD, and all flesh shall bless His holy name forever and ever."[181]

6. Personal Canon Prayer

The conditions of every person are different from

---

179   Psalms 100:2, 4.

180   Psalms 104:34.

181   Psalms 145:21.

those of others, whether on the spiritual level, or in the degree of mental and physical maturity, or concerning the educational and work-related situation, or regarding social status, and so on. Therefore, the Church has arranged that there be a father of confession who is responsible for determining the magnitude of the canon suitable for every one of his sons and daughters. The magnitude may be re-specified as the conditions of each confessant change. For example, the canon for the young man studying in university is different in magnitude from his canon after he graduates and has a job with specific hours, where now he has a new life routine. And the canon for the one who has a physical job, which is strenuous and extends for long hours in the day, is different from the magnitude of his canon if he were to pass—by God's permission—through a period of unemployment, while looking for another job. And perhaps this period may extend, in which case he needs more prayers, so that he may not fall into deadly idleness. For the fathers say that "the idle mind is the workshop of the devil."

The canon of each of us must consist of prayers from the Agpeya and psalms, for they are the foundation of the spiritual canon.

Let us take as an example the one who wrote the psalms, David the prophet, who said, "Seven times a day I praise You, because of Your righteous judgments,"[182] despite being a king and being busy with the affairs of the whole kingdom—with the many wars it contained—keeping in mind that at that time the king was responsible for judgment and ruling in conflicts and cases which the people presented to him.

Likewise is Daniel the prophet also. He was the second man in an enormous empire, representing most of the countries of the entire ancient world, and he was also entrusted with critical and sensitive duties; nevertheless, he had his own canon of prayer, worshipping, and thanksgiving, which he fulfilled daily at a specific time. And because of this canon itself, he was cast into the den of lions; then God revealed His glory through him: "Now when Daniel knew that the writing was signed, he went home. And in his upper room, with his windows open toward Jerusalem, he knelt down on his knees three times that day, and prayed and gave thanks before his God, as was his custom since early days."[183]

It was also said concerning the disciples that they were diligent in keeping the prayer in its appointed times, and they used to fulfill it in the temple as much as possible. In the Book of Acts, when the miracle was mentioned, of the healing of the man who was lame in front of the gate of the temple, Peter and John were chiefly going for the sake of the

---

182   Psalms 119:164.

183   Daniel 6:10.

ninth hour prayer at its appointed time: "Now Peter and John went up together to the temple at the hour of prayer, the ninth hour."[184]

It is possible for two or more people to share together in the personal canon prayer, in the case that their conditions be similar, and they agree together, as the Roman saints, Maximus and Dometius did, and as did the saints Abram and George. And numerous are the married couples who do so at their home, and also many of the brothers and spiritual friends, and some of the serious monks for the sake of encouraging each other, and this is done under the guidance of their elders.

It is also not necessary for you to fulfill your canon in the same location every day. Rather, in any place you happen to be, you can fulfill your canon, whether you are on a trip, or on a mission for service, or on a work-related assignment, or any other place. For when you possess persistence and determination, you will not be overcome by hindrances and obstacles.

The canon is then like a vow to God, which is our duty to perform day by day and forever, as the psalmist used to do: "So I will sing praise to Your name forever, that I may daily perform my vows."[185] Unfaithfulness in fulfilling the canon does not only sever our relationship with God, it also opens the

---

184 Acts 3:1.

185 Psalms 61:8.

door to the Devil, to attack us easily and exercise dominion over us.

The Christian, when praying with faithfulness and love for God, casts all his pains and troubles before God, as the Scripture says, "Cast your burden on the LORD."[186] We cannot do this in truth except by prayer. For he who believes that the Lord lifts up the burdens with all their heavy weight, and he trusts that God never permits a trial that is beyond their endurance, then he remains immovable with courage and patience before the battles, no matter how fierce they grow. And he cries out in his prayers, asking for assistance from his God, taking shelter in Him through his tears and prostrations, until he finally obtains consolation and peace. And all the bonds of Satan are loosed from him, with which he attempted to deceive him, to cast him into despair and hopelessness. Therefore, through prayer we can never fail. For there is nothing which prayer is not capable of.

How do I face the feeling of boredom and routine during the spiritual canon prayer?

Many of us perhaps complain of feeling bored and complain of the routine during the recitation of the canon. But be assured, brethren, that even the greatest saints pass through this warfare in their lives. Also this feeling is not at all an excuse to cease

---

186   Psalms 55:22.

from fulfilling the canon and neglecting it. Neither is it a reason for changing the quantity of the canon.

Facing this warfare is accomplished through forcefulness, patience, and perfect faithfulness in performing our promises and vows before God. For as there are vessels which are consecrated and dedicated for the altar service, and they cannot be used for any other purpose except the service, so also each one of us should consecrate and dedicate time from our day completely for God. And we should not do any other work except prayer during this time. For the day we are living now is a gift given to us by God. When God sees your labor, your faithfulness, your patience, and your struggle in prayer, even when you are passing through the warfare of boredom and distraction, He will certainly bestow upon you more grace, and give you consolation, joy, and peace finally. The same thing applies also to the dedication of a day in the week, to be the Lord's Day.

In *The Paradise of the Holy Fathers* and in the accounts of the lives of the saints, we find disciples complaining to their elders and their spiritual fathers about boredom and the distraction of the mind during the recitation of the canon and the prayers appointed for them. The following are some of the answers of the saints to their children.

Abba Paphnutius said, "Patience in prayer leads to great results; and negligence, which is given by the devil to men, leads to sluggishness of soul and its darkness, and [leads] men to falling into error and straying away from God, and [leads to] the captivity of the mind."[187]

Abba Paphnutius also said, "Persevering in Prayer is based on steadfastness, whether that is in the duration or patience, according to what is written, 'I have restrained myself like a woman in labor,'[188] that is, steadfastness in trials. And persevering in prayer, whether it is with many prayers or few, is considered a prayer with perseverance from the moment in which it is accompanied by labor. And this is a proof of steadfastness and persistence."[189]

Abba Macarius the Great also has the following important and beneficial sayings regarding this matter.

Abba Macarius said, "If you do not have the prayer of the spirit, strive for the prayer of the body, and then shall be added unto you the prayer in the spirit…. For it is written, 'Ask, and you shall receive' (Matthew 7:7)."[190]

---

187 *Bostan Al-Rohban Al-Mowasah, Al-joz' Al-Awal* [The Expanded Paradise of the Monks, Vol. 1]. (Egypt: St. Macarius Monastery, 2006), 363.

188 Cf. Isaiah 42:14.

189 *Bostan Al-Rohban Al-Mowasah, Al-joz' Al-Awal* [The Expanded Paradise of the Monks, Vol. 1]. (Egypt: St. Macarius Monastery, 2006), 367.

190 *The Paradise of the Holy Fathers* 2, A.W. Budge, trans. (London, UK: Chatto & Windus, 1907), 192.

And he said:

The one who adheres to prayer has acquired the best works. For it consequently needs greater struggle than the rest of the works. Also he must be exceedingly careful, be patient, and always labor, for the evil one is hostile to him, bringing upon him drowsiness, laziness, heaviness of body, relaxation, boredom, various thoughts, distraction of mind, and many tricks, to abolish it. For he needs to struggle unto bloodshed against those who seek to distance the soul from God. Let him watch and be alert with his mind, and insistently expel the hindering thought, and seek help from God.[191]

He also said:

The soul is obliged, at the time of psalmody, with compunction to collect its thoughts that wander aimlessly here and there—just as a mother gathers her children—even if they are going to be scattered again by sin, and to wait on the Lord with sure faith, so that He might come to it and teach it true

---

191 *Bostan Al-Rohban Al-Mowasah, Al-joz' Al-Awal* [The Expanded Paradise of the Monks, Vol. 1]. (Egypt: St. Macarius Monastery, 2006), 285–286.

prayer, and so that, undistracted by various thoughts, it might seek only the Lord.[192]

7. Unceasing Prayer

Unceasing prayer is a biblical commandment, which the Lord Christ Himself commanded us, saying, "Men always ought to pray and not lose heart."[193] So how do I combine prayer and my works, responsibilities, and commitments, which I must perform in my life?

Prayer is a relationship and connection with God, and our relationship and connection with God should be unceasing, and not only at the appointed times of prayer. And no one should think that he can combine between connection with God and connection with the world, its desires, and its pleasures, at the same time. For the Scripture is explicit about this exact point. Let us take an example of what the Lord Christ said in His sermon on the mount: "No one can serve two masters; for either he will hate the one and love the other, or else he will be loyal to the one and despise the other. You cannot serve God and mammon."[194]

---

192 *The Evergetinos* 4, Archbishop Chrysostomos and Hieromonk Patapios, trans. (Etna, CA: Center for Traditionalist Orthodox Studies, 2008), 155.

193 Luke 18:1.

194 Matthew 6:24.

This does not mean that we should leave our work and responsibilities, and completely devote ourselves to worshipping God. Rather, we must remain connected with God while we are performing all our works, and we should not lose the sense of always being in the presence of God wherever we are, and at any time in our life. Nevertheless, we should observe and sanctify the appointed and canonical times of worship, whether individual or communal.

Abba Anthony commands us, saying, "Whatever you are doing, have a testimony from Holy Scripture to hand."[195]

The Christian then takes God with him in his work, study, travels, going out and coming in, and all the aspects of his life; and this is so "that his deeds may be clearly seen, that they have been done in God."[196]

Even times for entertainment and casual conversations, with respect to the Christian, must have a spiritual character, which is completely at odds with the ways of the people of the world who do not walk according to the commandment of the Holy Scriptures. Their aim is love, which is God Himself, as our teacher St. Paul the Apostle commands us, saying, "… if any comfort of love."[197]

---

195 *Give Me a Word: The Alphabetical Sayings of the Desert Fathers*, J. Wortley, trans. (Yonkers, NY: SVS Press, 2014), Anthony 3.

196 John 3:21.

197 Philippians 2:1.

That is, God is in our midst, present with us in them [that is, in our times for entertainment].

When the Lord Christ commanded us that we ought to pray always and not lose heart, He gave us two parables: the parable of the widow and the unjust judge, and the parable of the Pharisee and the tax collector.

We have previously spoken about the necessity of persistence in prayer, after we talked about the story of the widow and the unjust judge. As for the parable of the Pharisee and the tax collector, the Church derived from it the phrase of his humble prayer, full of reverence, adding to it the name of Jesus Christ, thereby becoming, "Lord Jesus Christ, Son of God, have mercy on me, a sinner."[198]

This prayer became the arrow prayer known as the Jesus Prayer, and the believer is made to repeat it unceasingly, as much as possible, while performing all his works and his daily routine, so that God may be present with him in all his works and pursuits, thereby his life becomes sanctified.

There is another approach, which the fathers taught us, and is considered complementary to the Jesus Prayer: When we do any daily routine work, or fulfill the necessary needs of the body, of eating, drinking, washing the hands, bathing, and so on, we ought to recite during this [activity] a suitable verse from the Holy Scriptures, which we had committed

198   Cf. Luke 18:13.

to memory for this purpose. In the beginning, some people write the suitable verses on small pieces of paper and glue them in their own place where they are accustomed to doing the action the verse expresses. Here are some examples.

When I wake up from sleep, I say, "I lay down and slept; I awoke, for the LORD sustained me,"[199] or, "As for me, I will see Your face in righteousness; I shall be satisfied when I awake in Your likeness."[200]

When I wash my face, I seek the face of the One who is fairer than the sons of men, to see His image in my face, saying, "When You said, 'Seek My face,' my heart said to You, 'Your face, LORD, I will seek.'"[201] Or I hope in God, thanking Him and saying to myself, "Hope in God; for I shall yet praise Him, the help of my countenance and my God."[202]

When I wash my hands, I say, "I will wash my hands in innocence."[203] This is the same verse which the priest recites when he washes his hands during the Divine Liturgy, adding the following remaining words, "So I will go about Your altar, O LORD."[204]

When I bathe, I recite, saying, "Purge me with hyssop, and I shall be clean; wash me, and I shall

---

199 Psalms 3:5.

200 Psalms 17:15.

201 Psalms 27:8.

202 Psalms 42:11.

203 Psalms 26:6.

204 Ibid.

be whiter than snow."[205] Some might recite the rest of the psalm, and might repeat it many times consecutively until they finish bathing, for most Christians have this psalm committed to memory.

When I am putting on my clothes, I remember the saying of our teacher Paul the Apostle, that I may sow my entire day with love for all: "Put on love, which is the bond of perfection."[206] And perhaps I want to continue, saying, "For as many of you as were baptized into Christ have put on Christ."[207] Or I may prefer to say, "My soul shall be joyful in my God; for He has clothed me with the garments of salvation, He has covered me with the robe of righteousness."[208]

When I go out of my house, I cannot do without these two verses: "The LORD shall preserve you from all evil; He shall preserve your soul. The LORD shall preserve your going out and your coming in from this time forth, and even forevermore."[209] Some might add after this and say, "Lord, what do You want me to do?"[210] "O LORD, truly I am Your servant,"[211] "do to us whatever seems best to You,"[212]

---

205 Psalms 51:7. Psalm 50 in LXX.

206 Colossians 3:14.

207 Galatians 3:27.

208 Isaiah 61:10.

209 Psalms 121:7–8.

210 Acts 9:6.

211 Psalms 116:16.

212 Judges 10:15.

"that I might not sin against You."[213]

For each work in life, there must be something suitable for it from the Holy Scriptures. And let us remember that the Lord Christ was a Man like us, who "resembled us in everything, except for sin alone."[214] And He Himself fought the devil and defeated him by this method, and He gave it to us, so that we may follow His example during our life on earth.

Thus also through the holy word of God, man's life is sanctified in its entirety, and a person remains continuously in contact with God.

And not only is man sanctified by prayer, but also the matter we use in our lives is sanctified, and our use of it becomes for the glory of God, and for thanking Him, and for declaring His power and wisdom. "For every creature of God is good, and nothing is to be refused if it is received with thanksgiving; for it is sanctified by the word of God and prayer."[215] And when we become accustomed to giving thanks always, before and after any action or work, prayer becomes the first and last work we do and a means to sanctify everything in our whole life.

When you buy a new car, for example, or a new house, you ask a priest to come and pray and bless

---

213 Psalms 119:11.

214 The Divine Liturgy According to Saint Gregory – Prayer of Reconciliation.

215 1 Timothy 4:4–5.

it. Why? So that it may be sanctified. As St. Paul the Apostle says to his disciple Timothy, "For it is sanctified by the word of God and prayer."[216]

There is a possibility for physical matter to be sanctified by prayer and the word of God. Therefore also, before you eat your meal, you pray and make the sign of the cross, and by this the food you are eating is sanctified. And when you drink a cup of tea, you sign it with the sign of the cross and say, "Bless, Lord," and this is so that it may be sanctified. The same thing you do when you take your medications or eat sweets. You pray, bless, and thank God, and you trust that what you are taking has become sanctified.

As for the time of conversation with others, we must take the greatest care in this, so that the spirit of prayer, which we acquired in the moments of stillness, may not abandon us. Concerning this our teacher Paul the Apostle directs us, saying, "Let your speech always be with grace, seasoned with salt, that you may know how you ought to answer each one."[217] That is, let our speech always be in agreement with the Spirit of God who is in us, and with the life of prayer which we live. And this is so that we do not break it off during our conversation. And I wish that during our conversation we always quote verses from the Holy Scriptures or the sayings

216 Ibid.
217 Colossians 4:6.

of the holy fathers, such holy words which give grace to the hearers and make mutual understanding in speech easy to reach. As for the second mile in a conversation, it is to turn to what the Lord Jesus said to us in His sermon on the mount: "But let your 'Yes' be 'Yes,' and your 'No,' 'No.' For whatever is more than these is from the evil one."[218]

The meaning of this is that in addition to our commitment to the words of our mouths before others, we must also talk less as much as possible, so long as speaking will not edify or benefit, for "in the multitude of words sin is not lacking, but he who restrains his lips is wise."[219] And well did Abba Arsenius, the tutor of the Emperor's sons, say, "I often repented of having spoken, never of remaining silent."[220]

Let us be careful and always remember the divine judgment which said, "But I say to you that for every idle word men may speak, they will give account of it in the day of judgment."[221] For this reason, the virtue of silence is considered one of the greatest virtues that leads to the unceasing prayer of the heart.

---

218 Matthew 5:37.

219 Proverbs 10:19.

220 *Give Me a Word: The Alphabetical Sayings of the Desert Fathers*, J. Wortley, trans. (Yonkers, NY: SVS Press, 2014), Arsenius 40.

221 Matthew 12:36.

8

Praying to the Holy Trinity

We should have a relationship with the Father and the Son and the Holy Spirit, as the Church teaches us through her prayers.

When we meditate on the liturgical prayers of the Church, we find that there are prayers that are directed to the Father, like the Thanksgiving Prayer, the Divine Liturgy According to St. Basil, which the Church uses most of the year, and the Lord's Prayer, "Our Father who art in heaven." And some of these prayers conclude with "in Christ Jesus our Lord," as the Lord Jesus Christ Himself commanded us, saying, "Most assuredly, I say to you, whatever you ask the Father in My name He will give you."[222]

There are other prayers that are directed to the Son, like the Divine Liturgy According to St. Gregory, and the litanies in the Agpeya prayers,

---

222 John 16:23.

which say, "O You, who on the sixth day and in the sixth hour were nailed to the cross…" and, "O You, who tasted death in the flesh in the ninth hour."

Let us also note that nearly half of the absolutions at the end of every hour in the Agpeya are directed to the Father, while the other half to the Son. As for the middle of the day, in the absolution of the ninth hour, we find that half of it is directed to the Father, while the second half to the Son.

There are prayers that are directed to the Holy Spirit throughout the Divine Liturgy, calling upon Him to sanctify both us and the gifts set forth upon the Altar. There is also another prayer that is the fourth litany in the third hour of the Agpeya: "O heavenly King, the Comforter…"

There are prayers and praises that are directed to the Holy Trinity, like the Trisagion prayer, and "Holy, Holy, Holy" at the conclusion of every hour, and in the praises of Koiahk and the distribution hymns.

The Lord Christ has come to teach us how to worship and serve the Father in Spirit and truth. "No one has seen God at any time. The only begotten Son, who is in the bosom of the Father, He has declared Him."[223] That is, the Lord Christ has come to declare God the Father to us, so that we may be able to enter into a relationship with God the Father, and He spoke to us about Him, saying,

223 John 1:18.

"For the Father Himself loves you, because you have loved Me, and have believed that I came forth from God."[224]

God the Father has sent His only begotten Son, Jesus Christ, that the Son may reconcile us to the Father, concerning which St. Paul the Apostle says, "Who has reconciled us to Himself through Jesus Christ."[225]

Christ has also come to teach us how to pray to God the Father, saying, "Until now you have asked nothing in My name. Ask, and you will receive, that your joy may be full."[226] Therefore, all our prayers which are directed to the Father must be in the name of Jesus Christ, as the Church concludes the Lord's Prayer.

And at the same time, the Lord Christ encourages us to have a true relationship, not only with the Father, but also with the Holy Spirit, whom He promised to send to us, saying, "But when the Helper comes, whom I shall send to you from the Father, the Spirit of truth who proceeds from the Father, He will testify of Me,"[227] and, "But the Helper, the Holy Spirit, whom the Father will send in My name, He will teach you all things, and bring

---

224 John 16:27.

225 2 Corinthians 5:18.

226 John 16:24.

227 John 15:26.

to your remembrance all things that I said to you."[228]

Then my beloved, we must examine our relationship with God the Holy Trinity, to have a connection with the Father and the Son and the Holy Spirit. And by this, we will have a true relationship with the Holy Trinity.

---

228 John 14:26.

9

How Do I Rejoice and be Joyful in Prayer?

1. The Prayer of the Second Mile

Many come to me and ask me, saying, "What is the minimum prayers that I must pray in my own spiritual canon? And what is the minimum number of Liturgies, Vespers prayers, and gatherings, that I must attend? And what is the minimum in the service that I must do? And what is the minimum struggle with which I can enter heaven?"

Such people consider prayer an obligation that they must do. They want to fulfill it only to ease their conscience; then they occupy the rest of their time with the affairs of the world and its pleasures. Such as those, though they may be in the first stages of spiritual infancy in prayer, rarely receive consolation, and they do not desire to grow spiritually and do not understand the true meaning of prayer.

Prayer, as we have previously said, is a connection and communication with God. For we are the ones who need it so that we may receive consolation and joy through it; and so that we may be qualified by it to unite with our Creator and receive forgiveness for our mistakes, iniquities, and all kinds of sins; and so that by it also we may have boldness with Him, that we may be able to place our supplications before Him; and on top of all this, so that we may have a pledge to the heavenly inheritance in His everlasting Kingdom.

Therefore, the priest prays to God in the Divine Liturgy, saying, "You had no need of my servitude, but rather I had need of Your lordship."[229]

We need the connection and communication with our Creator, that we may express our love and gratitude to Him, not only for all that He did and will do with us throughout our life here, but also because He will open to us His fatherly bosom, that we may live with Him in eternity, the life of continuous joy, where "there shall be no more death, nor sorrow, nor crying. There shall be no more pain, for the former things have passed away,"[230] and where "eye has not seen, nor ear heard, nor have

---

229 The Divine Liturgy According to Saint Gregory – Agios (holy).
230 Revelation 21:4.

entered into the heart of man the things which God has prepared for those who love Him."[231]

Therefore, why do we insist on doing the least struggle in prayer? And why do we make our goal to have the minimum communication with our Creator?

One of the fathers explained this matter in a nice way, as follows. Let us presume that there was a straight line, named the line of spiritual struggle in prayer. The area to the right side of this line is the love of God and the relationship with Him, while the area to the left is the love of the world and the attachment to it. We may be surprised that most Christians remain for a long time eager to be near this line. For either they do not desire to delve deeper into the area to the right, that is the love of God, and so some remain attached to this line on the right side, so that they may be near to the delights of the world; or some may be eager to be most of the time on the line itself, yet from time to time they falter between the right and left; or others might remain near the line from the left side, for they are afraid of hell fire, yet at the same time they cannot give up their attachment to the world and its pleasures. And they think that they are able to cross to the other side at any time they want. But they are deceived in truth.

Beloved, the Christian life, which the Lord

---

231   1 Corinthians 2:9.

Christ came to teach us, is truly the life of the second mile, which is the mile of love or the mile of joy. It is also the mile of freedom. But even the entire Christian religion is called the religion of the second mile.

It is the mile of delivering oneself and sacrifice with one's freedom and the fullness of the will, as Christ Himself did, "who for the joy that was set before Him endured the cross, despising the shame."[232] He delivered Himself a living sacrifice on the cross, and He did not sin but did this for the sake of our sins. It was not obligatory for Him to do any of these things, but He accepted to give His life for our redemption. All this is for the joy that was set before Him, for the sake of our salvation and to take away the shame and punishment from us, for the sake of our return to paradise and to our first estate, for the sake of being one with Him and His Father and His Holy Spirit.[233]

He is a good God, full of love, and His love compels Him to give, deliver Himself, sacrifice, but even die for the sake of the ones whom He loves. He not only desires goodness for us, but also eternal joy, and clinging to Him, and sitting with Him on His throne to partake of His glory, and much more which we do not know and can never imagine or write down.

---

232 Hebrews 12:2.
233 See John 17:21.

This was the joy of Christ, to give us all these exceeding gifts, and we do not at all deserve any of them. For true joy comes after giving, and through sacrificing, with all love and freedom. Therefore, the Scripture says, "It is more blessed to give than to receive."[234]

If we are only satisfied with what is required of us in prayer, content with what we obtain from God for ourselves, we will neither grow nor rejoice, but will diminish, become bored, and grow lukewarm. We will never use prayer as a connection through which we call our Creator. If we restrict all prayers within the mere half an hour or hour which we spend before God, then this is not a [true] connection or relationship with Him.

The struggle of prayer requires of us the offering of the second mile, the mile with which we express our love for our Creator, offering it fully with our will, so that we may finally obtain the joy and peace which surpass all understanding. This mile is the mile of going into the deep, the right-side area of the love of God, with our entire will and freedom. It may require intensity and forcing oneself at the beginning, yet God has promised us that we will never fail if we choose the second mile with our entire will and freedom.[235] For "where the Spirit of the Lord is, there is liberty."[236]

---

234 Acts 20:35.

235 See 2 Corinthians 4:1.

236 2 Corinthians 3:17.

A nun came to me once and said to me, "To be honest with you, every day I go to Midnight Praises, feeling that I am forced to do this, because it is the rule of the monastery. I feel no consolation or joy throughout the Praises, but on the contrary I feel extremely troubled when I am going to Midnight Praises." I said to her, "You are not forced to wake up to go to Midnight Praises. But you must choose, by your free will, to attend Midnight Praises, saying to yourself, 'I am going to praise God, the Bridegroom of my heart, and not because this is the rule of the monastery. I am going by my entire freedom and will, to meet my Bridegroom and to express my love to Him.' As the psalm says, 'Serve the LORD with gladness; come before His presence with singing.... Enter into His gates with thanksgiving, and into His courts with praise. Be thankful to Him, and bless His name.'237" After some time she sent me a message, saying, "The power of choice has liberated me and brought about profound joy and peace in my heart. It made me go to Midnight Praises voluntarily, and I am joyful, feeling that I am the one who made the decision, and not because it is the rule of the monastery."

The gospel of the second mile gives joy and peace to man. And you too, my brethren, choose by yourselves and with all your freedom, to pour yourself completely before God, and not to offer to Him what is obligatory and that is it. Choose to be a

237 Psalms 100:2, 4.

man of prayer, being constantly in contact with God at all times, rejoicing with Him always. May God bless this connection for you, and make it grow and bear fruit, for His holy name.

2. Be an Intercessor, not a Judge

When we previously spoke about the intercession of the saints, we indicated quickly that we should imitate the lives of the saints during our struggle here on earth, in that we may intercede in our prayers for the sake of the weaknesses of our brethren, and not judge them and publicize their sins. Here we will briefly speak of how this matter can lead to joy and rejoicing during prayer.

St. Paul the Apostle says, "I thank my God upon every remembrance of you, always in every prayer of mine making request for you all with joy."[238] Here we see how Paul the Apostle, while praying and remembering the Philippians, used to make requests for them all with joy of heart.

God is not joyful by the one who accuses another and judges him, for this shows that he lacks love. Rather He is joyful by the one who loves others, and covers their weaknesses, and prays for them; therefore, He bestows upon him the gift of joy.

All the Holy Scriptures are summarized in two commandments, "You shall love the LORD your God

238 Philippians 1:3–4.

with all your heart.... And the second, like it, is this: 'You shall love your neighbor as yourself.' There is no other commandment greater than these."[239]

The heart that is full of love must necessarily be full of joy also, and these are the first two fruits of the nine known fruit of the Holy Spirit.[240] And both are tightly bound to each other, and they are the fruits that lead to the third fruit—that is, peace. This peace is unlike the peace of the world, rather it is the peace of God, which surpasses all understanding.

The person who has a loving heart, who expresses the depth of his love when he stands and struggles in prayers and supplications for the sake of the others' needs, has necessarily a heart devoid of hatred, selfishness, and ego; therefore, you find him always beaming with joy and in a state of peace. When we see two people who love each other, in harmony and intimacy, we conclude that they are in a state of inward and outward joy together, and this joy is the result of their love for each other.

Likewise, when you are in a state of love with God and with other people, you will always be in a state of joy. And there is no way or means that is more sublime and deeper, to obtain this love, then expressing it, and persisting and growing in it, than through prayer. Your love for God will make you

---

239 Mark 12:30–31.
240 See Galatians 5:22.

offer the prayers of the second mile to Him with joy; and your love for people will make you intercede for them before God with joy, as we saw Paul praying for the people of Philippi, and as we heard of the saints who were before us. And in this way, you will fulfill the commandments of all the Holy Scriptures in these two steps.

My brethren, you cannot then but cling to the love of prayer, for it is the connection of love and the source of joy, here in this life now and in the kingdom forever. Amen.